JOBS, INTERVIEWS, SUCCESS

Complete job advice for students

How to choose your career

How to land the job offer

Start treading the path to success

Neil Thompson

First published in 2005 by Management Books 2000 Ltd
Forge House, Limes Road
Kemble, Cirencester
Gloucestershire, GL7 6AD, UK
Tel: 0044 (0) 1285 771441
Fax: 0044 (0) 1285 771055
E-mail: info@mb2000.com
Web: www.mb2000.com

Printed and bound in Great Britain by Digital Book Print Ltd, MK1 1DR

British Library Cataloguing in Publication Data is available

ISBN 1-85252-482-0

JOBS, INTERVIEWS, SUCCESS

Contents

Part Three – Start Treading the Path to Success

Introduction

Some people wake up in the morning looking forward to the whole day. They can't wait to see their friends at work, to crack a few jokes over a coffee and to get into the latest issues.

Other people don't. They drag themselves out of bed, drive to work wishing that they were really going somewhere else.

Are the fortunate people simply lucky? The answer is no – they spent the time and effort needed to understand what they wanted and did the work that was necessary to get it.

The purpose of this book is to help you do the same.

Some people take jobs more or less at random. They take the first opening that happens to come along. They drift into jobs that are never going to work out for them, and they could have known that if they had thought a bit harder before they leapt in.

Choose your job – don't drift into it

Choosing gets you on the path to your dream. Drifting can leave you shouting for help.

The first part of the book shows you how to choose a job that will be right for you.

Once you have made your choice you have to get the job. That's what the second part is all about. Some people say that all you have to do for an interview is to wear a suit, turn up and be yourself. Would you prepare for your final exams by simply turning up and being yourself? Of course not – you would under-perform badly. You put in months of revision to make sure you can deliver your best performance on the day. The same is true for job interviews, preparation is crucial. Part Two of the book takes you through how to write your CV and prepare for your interview in detail.

And of course once you have found your job you have to find your feet and start treading the path to success – that's the third part of the book.

What are we waiting for? Let's get straight into the first section on how to make the right career choice.

Part One

How to Choose Your Career

1

Career Planning

Jobs are not good or bad. The right job for you is all about fit. If the person and the job fit together, then it's the right job – if they don't fit then it's not.

When you're in a job that fits, you feel full of energy and enthusiasm. You are pleased to see the people at work and you feel appreciated. When it doesn't fit, you spend most of the day looking at your watch to see if it's five o'clock yet. There's no energy or enthusiasm – you simply don't want to be there.

Sounds easy so far? Well here's the difficult bit. To predict a fit between you and your job we need to find a few things out:

1. **Who are you and what matters to you?** You need to know the answers in objective terms that you can feed into your career decisions;
2. You need to know **what the potential jobs are all about**, the reality, not the recruitment advertisements or company product brochures.

For most people these questions are not easy. We will take you through a structured method to help you answer them. Bear in mind that no one can simply tell you who you are or what you want. Some people and some books might try, but at the end of the day, it's your life and it's your decision.

What we can do is to show you all the right questions to ask and take you through our method so you can find your own answers and make a decision that's right for you.

Ask a friend

It can be easier and more likely to be successful if you go through the process with someone to help you. See if you can find a friend who is going through the same process, then you can both do it together.

There are so many ways to tackle questions about who you are and what you want. No single approach on its own is enough for you to make a decision. It's not enough to simply do what your friends are doing, or to do what you think will make the most money, or to tick some boxes on a test and believe the result. You need to look at all the answers together; you need to look at the big picture.

We do this using the **Career Decisions Model**. Your desires, talents, personality, external influences and your own dreams are taken into consideration.

It is a very big leap to go from your talents, interests and personality straight to job choices. There are important steps missing. We use the intermediate step of **'Job Activities'** to help you in your career choice. These are what you do at work on a day-to-day basis. Examples of common Job Activities are:

- doing detailed numerical calculations on your PC
- meeting people and helping them
- telling people what to do.

Satisfaction, energy, fulfilment and enjoyment come from what you actually do each hour of each day and from the people with whom you work. These wonderful things come from an employee fitting well with the Job Activities that he or she does.

Job descriptions and stereotypes can be very deceptive; what we might expect from a job can be very different from what people actually do there on a day-to-day basis. Looking at the activities involved in a job can give a much better idea of the reality of the job day-to-day and hour-to-hour.

Job Activities are not industry or job specific. You can find the same or very similar activities across a wide range of jobs in different industries.

To have the best chance of choosing the right job for you we first find the Job Activities that fit you. Only then can you look objectively at jobs to see if what you will be doing day-to-day will suit you. You can then bring in all the other factors that come into a career decision to pick the right job.

Let's look at a couple of examples:

1 You're interested in food and you think about being a chef

Thinking about food is wonderful. Eating it is even better. It is logical that someone who is interested in food might want to become a chef. Let's look at the Job Activities of a chef:

- creates a menu to attract customers and sell meals (or is told what to cook)
- experiments with new recipes (or is told what to cook)
- buys food
- prepares ingredients (on your feet, scrubbing, peeling, weighing etc)
- can be ordered around quite strictly by the head chef
- multi-tasks (has many things on the go at once)
- works in a mini-crisis much of the time
- cooks large volumes as quickly as is reasonable
- is on his or her feet most of the time and works late into the night
- does not get on TV or meet Jamie Oliver unless he or she is incredibly good and incredibly lucky
- as a sous-chef, spends the time tidying, sterilising, cleaning and putting away as well. It is very hard work.

These are the activities the would-be chef needs to consider. Can he or she enjoy these activities? Liking food is not enough. Finding a fit with the Job Activities of a Chef is much more likely to lead to a good decision.

2 You're thinking about becoming a lawyer

We have all seen glamourous TV shows involving lawyers. They are usually in court making righteous speeches and 'winning'. It's all about charisma and performance. In the UK, a very small percentage of lawyers work as barristers. The majority are solicitors or business legal advisors. Here are some of a lawyer's activities:

- studying and remembering legislation and previous cases
- paying incredibly detailed attention to language and words
- drafting and reviewing detailed contracts
- reading through hundreds of pages to find one crucial sentence
- working long hours
- selling his or her own time and looking after clients
- proof reading contracts
- filing and organising papers and electronic files.

Lawyers are detail people. Good language ability, good preparation and attention to detail make a good lawyer. Have you ever seen the TV series *Ally McBeal*? Ally is attractive, intelligent and stylish but she's not much of a realist and she's forgetful. In the real world she would probably be an awful lawyer. Her boss John – 'the funny little man' – is meticulous, socially awkward and introverted. He checks that his collar and tie are straight three times before he leaves the bathroom. He would probably make an excellent lawyer.

You should be able to see from the examples that what you actually do in a particular job can be quite different from the reputation and image that a job might have. Find the Job Activities that suit you and then choose the job – that way you have much more chance of finding work that you genuinely enjoy.

To choose suitable Job Activities (JAs) we look at the following areas:

- what you're good at
- what you like doing
- your personality and temperament
- previous experience that you have.

When you have a good idea about the JAs that suit you, then you're in a position to look at the other factors that go into a job decision. We look at:

- your original dreams or ambitions
- influence of your parents
- your qualifications
- previous experience
- people with whom you work
- trends in the employment market
- the money, status and lifestyle you want.

Here's a diagram of the Career Decisions Model to show you how it all fits together.

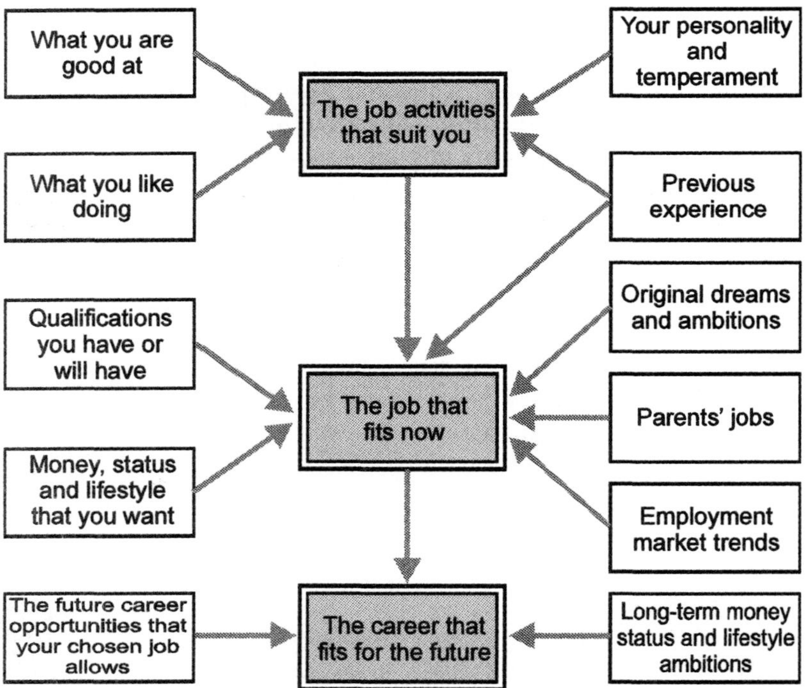

Career Decisions Model

Summary – career planning

☑ Choose your career – don't drift into it. And choose it intelligently.

☑ Use the methods given to look carefully into who you are and what you want and then find a job that fits.

☑ Very few jobs are good or bad. They fit you or they don't fit you.

☑ To find fit we need to look at Job Activities that are right for you.

☑ Then you bring in all the other influences of a career decision and choose the job that will fit you.

☑ Get under the skin of the jobs that interest you. That's the only way you can make an intelligent informed decision. That's the only way you can get it right.

Next ➔➔

So let's start the process of finding the Job Activities that suit you. When we know more about your Job Activities, we will be in a position to talk about jobs themselves.

2

Starting to Find Your Job Activities

In this chapter we look at what you are good at, what you like and any previous experience that you have had. It's a chapter where you have to do some thinking. Take your time over it. Some people find it helpful to go through the process twice or a few times. Get a pencil out now.

Have you got a pencil in your hand? Or did you read that sentence and think that you'd do it later or it doesn't really apply to you. If you're reading the book then it does apply to you and you probably won't do it later. Get the pencil. The benefit of this chapter comes from the things you write down.

And don't forget to enjoy yourself – this chapter is a mini journey within yourself – have a good trip.

What you are good at

You should already have a feel for what you are good at and what you're not so good at. There will be school and maybe university subjects where you perform(ed) better. Note these down here. It's not whether you liked them, just what you did best in.

My best school/university subjects are/were:

Write down anything else that you feel you do well. Simple things can be really important; they don't have to be high-flown business topics. And don't worry if you're not sure they're relevant, write them all down.

Other things I do well are:

If you had trouble identifying what you think you are good at, don't worry. The section on personality and temperament and how it relates to activities will help.

You can take a formal aptitude test if you feel that you really don't know what you do or could do well. A common one is the Differential Aptitude Test (DAT). It tests your aptitude in the following areas: verbal reasoning, numerical ability, abstract reasoning, clerical speed and accuracy, mechanical reasoning, spatial aptitude, spelling, language usage. Contact your local careers centre if you feel you would benefit from an aptitude test.

What you like doing

Now go through a similar exercise to the one above, but think about activities you *like or feel comfortable* doing rather than things that you are good at. Just write down anything that differs from the list of things you are good at.

Here's an example. I enjoyed Art at school – but I was an awful painter. I was top of the class in Physics and near the bottom in Art. However, I enjoyed it, and there's important information for me there. I love to be creative and I don't enjoy work unless there is an element of creativity. Being creative is definitely one of my Job Activities. (I still paint sometimes, the results are awful as ever but I love doing it just like I did at school).

What subjects did or do you like at school or university?

Subjects I like(d) at school/university are:

Now note down anything else that you know you like doing – whether it's business related or not. (Don't write Sex, Drugs and Rock and Roll; we're not covering those industries here! Well, maybe Rock and Roll).

Other activities I enjoy are:

You can take a formal test for your interests or motivation. If you are keen on tests then an interest test can be useful. A common interests test is the Strong Interest Inventory. Contact your local careers centre for more information.

Previous experience

You may have previous work experience. What were you doing there? Try to identify the Job Activities that were involved.

And here is the question – did you enjoy the activities? Did you look forward to the next day? If you did, then that's the real confirmation that they are good activities for you.

JAs I can identify from previous work experience are:

The ones I particularly enjoyed and/or did well are:

Was your experience a summer job? Quite a few people find summer jobs a bit less enjoyable than they had expected and can be put off that line of work. If you're in this position, then think carefully about the activities that you were actually doing in your summer job. It can be hard for companies to involve summer employees in the real work that's going on when they are only there for a number of weeks. Summer workers often sit around waiting to do the filing or answer the phone. These are probably very different JAs from those you would be involved in if you had a full time job. Think as well about the activities that the full-time employees were involved in. Would you have enjoyed them more?

Chapter two summary

- ☑ To find a job that fits you need to be clear about who you are and what you want. These are difficult questions. We've been through some exercises to help you think about it.
- ☑ Did you actually get a pen out and write some answers down? If not then go back and do it now.
- ☑ Other people can try to tell you what you want, but they don't have as much chance of getting it right as you do. The best that others can do is to help you to find your own answers.
- ☑ You have now started to identify your preferred Job Activities. These are what you like and what you are good at described in a way that is directly relevant to professional employment.
- ☑ They are the major stepping-stone towards finding the job that is right for you.
- ☑ Well done!

Next ➔➔

The next section is about personality. It's another pointer towards the right JAs for you.

3

Personality and Temperament

Introduction

People have very different personalities. We all know a wide range of characters amongst our friends and associates. Some might be really sociable and always want to meet new people and others may be more comfortable alone or with people they know very well. Some people are very organised and regimented and others are more spontaneous or even chaotic. Some are naturally in tune with other peoples' feelings and others might be more interested in logic.

Think about the cast of *Star Trek* (The Next Generation for this example). It's quite interesting in terms of personality even if you don't like *Star Trek*. The scriptwriters have separated out a few personality traits and built a whole character around each one. That makes it easy for us to identify personally with the characters very quickly. Then they play each character (or personality trait) off against the others.

Data, the android, is purely logical, he hasn't got any feelings, whereas Diana Troy, the ship's counsellor, is empathetic to the crew's feelings to the point that she is telepathic. She doesn't have to ask how they are – she already knows. Captain Packard is the master of authority and decisions and Number One is the centre of all the action.

What would happen if you asked Data to do Diana Troy's job as a counsellor? It would be a disaster. An emotionally troubled crew member would come to him asking for understanding and all he would do would be to lecture them on the logical basis of psychological theory from his memory banks. When Data talks to Troy he always comes away puzzled. 'Interesting' he says, as if each of her counselling cases could be a nice logical challenge for him.

If Diana Troy were asked to lead an Away Team on a dangerous mission she would probably spend so much time making sure that everyone felt all right that they might not actually achieve very much. And she'd be stressed out as well because she'd be able to feel that she wasn't really suited to the task. Afterwards she might say to Number One, 'But how can you expect the ship's soldiers to risk their lives on a mission if they don't feel it's right?'

Obviously we need to talk about reality, not TV shows – but the concept is the same in our work. We have natural traits in our personalities that will mean we are better suited to some roles than others. If you are well suited to a role then you will enjoy it more, and almost certainly do better in it.

We can all work in jobs that don't really suit us and still be successful for a while. Determination can take people a long way, but it's stressful and there's not much job satisfaction. Long-term performance and even health can suffer. You are unlikely to have a successful long-term career in work that doesn't suit you.

Let's look at some personality theory first, and then see how it can affect the type of Job Activities that are right for you.

Personality type – introduction

A quick caution first. Dealing with personality and personality tests can be a bit dangerous. It's complex stuff and it takes expertise and experience to use personality tests reliably. Think of them a bit like fireworks – there's no problem if you let someone else do the work and take in what happens. Then there's an intermediate stage where you start to mess about with them yourself and it can be dangerous, but the for the experts there's no problem.

In a chapter this size we can get to the point where you can see what the subject's about and have some interesting ideas to feed into the Career Decisions Model – you can watch the firework show, but don't base your decision solely on the personality information in this chapter. Let the information compliment the other factors that come into your decision.

There are shortened versions of personality tests that you can take on your own. You can find them on the internet or in books. Doing these can be like messing about with fireworks. The short versions are not very reliable and there is no one to explain the theory or to interpret the results properly. They can lead you to conclusions that aren't true. The results can be quite misleading to people who take them sincerely.

When you have finished reading this chapter, if you're interested in the subject and feel that it is a big help to you, then we suggest two things. First get a book called *'Do What You Are'* by an American couple called the Tiegers. You can find it on Amazon.com. It gives a good introduction to personality type in the context of careers. Then take a full-length test with an official administrator. Make sure that he or she spends time explaining the whole topic and specifically what personality you are and what that means for various careers that you are interested in. There are various tests available – we recommend the Myers Briggs Type Indicator.

Personality theory

We use a model that has eight basic personality traits; it's a simplified model based on work derived from the Swiss psychologist, Jung. We give descriptions of some typical behaviour or thinking in each trait. Some of the phrases will be familiar to you – you could use them to describe yourself, and others won't be like you at all. Note down the traits where you read the familiar phrases. They come in pairs. You should be able to see if you are more like A or B in each pair. Don't think about what you should be, there is no right or wrong or good or bad. Think about who you are, and be proud of it! You can also ask someone else who knows you well to read through the descriptions and to suggest how you fit in with them.

Imagine each pair of descriptions as a line between two extremes. You can be anywhere on the line, at one end or the other, or if you feel you can't decide between two descriptions or you see yourself on both sides then you can sit right in the middle.

1 – Introvert or Extrovert

1A Extroverts E

You like being the centre of the group.
You like to talk.
You feel good when there are lots of people around.
Sitting at home reading is not your favourite pastime, you would usually rather be with some friends or out at a party.
You prefer to work in groups rather than alone.
You like to try a wide variety of things.

1B Introverts I

You like to work alone; you can find other people bothersome when you're working.
You like to read and consider your thoughts.
Polite conversations at parties can be trivial.
You think issues through before blurting out an opinion.
You prefer to understand a few things deeply rather than gloss over lots of different topics.

Circle the one that sounds more like you. Circle – I or E

Be careful with the stereotype of introverts and extroverts. It's easy to think that introverts are boring and extroverts are interesting and cool – that's not the case. It's just where you find your energy, from within or from other people. Introverted doesn't mean you can't deal with other people.

2 Detail or Big Picture

2A Detail People D

You notice all the details and information around you.
People would describe you as a realist.
You think about the present, what's going on now.
You like concrete evidence and facts.
You can't stand mistakes and go to great lengths to avoid them.

You do things step by step.

2B Big Picture Thinkers **B**

You love imagination; you often have your own movie or scene going on in your head.
You think about the future.
New tasks are interesting, and you might get bored with old issues or tasks.
You trust your instinct or your sixth sense.
You prefer the big picture to the fine print. You take the overall view.
You are an 'ideas person'.

Which of these is more like you? Circle – D or B

3 – Logical Thinker or Follow Your Heart

3A Logical Thinker **L**

You apply logic to a problem or situation before anything else.
You make decisions based on the facts even if the outcome might upset other people.
You write pros and cons down and weigh them up.
Truth is more important than tact.
You value justice; the same rules apply to everyone.
You don't mind telling people what to do, but you might be a bit abrupt and upset them sometimes.

3B Follow Your Heart **H**

If you come to a decision point you sleep on it and see how you feel about it in the morning.
You like harmony; you like to please others.
You can get quite emotional.
You want to be appreciated by the people around you.
You always try to be tactful, even if someone is obviously out of line.
You feel awkward telling people what to do. What if they don't like it?

Do you think you are a Logical Thinker or do you Follow Your Heart?
Circle – L or H

4 – Structured or Free

4A Structured S

You take deadlines seriously.

You like to get things finished.

You like your work and your life to be organised, so you know exactly what you're doing.

You work hard and only take time off when the job is finished.

You set goals for yourself.

You are always aware of time.

4B Free F

You don't mind changing a deadline if you need to.

You enjoy doing a task for the fun of it; the satisfaction is not just in finishing it.

You like starting new things.

You don't like life to be too strictly organised, you can take things as they come.

Some people are obsessed by punctuality – you're not.

You like to have free time where you can do whatever you want to.

Which of these is more like you? Circle – S or F

Summarise your choices below. You might relate strongly to the descriptions in one of the traits in one pair and then find it difficult to distinguish between the next pair. That's normal, some traits appear very strongly and others less so. If you felt quite strongly about one of the descriptions then note down which one it was.

The descriptions that fit me best are:

1	**Extrovert**	**Introvert**
2	**Detail**	**Big Picture**
3	**Logical Thinker**	**Follow Your Heart**

4 Structured Free

The one(s) that I felt most strongly about are ________________

Case study

Let's go through a case so you can see how someone else recognised their personality from the descriptions. The case is about Nicola, a second year Computer Science student.

Extrovert or Introvert

She goes to a lot of parties, but usually sticks with the same group of friends. And to be honest, she'd be just as happy to meet them in someone's room and have a chat. She doesn't go to parties to talk to every person in the room.

She works hard with a lot of hours alone on her laptop and she doesn't mind doing it. In fact she needs to be alone to work, she finds it hard to work with a lot of interruptions. But after a few hours, she needs to get up and talk to someone. She loves sport – she's a good competitive swimmer, but she doesn't do twenty different sports to try them all out, she sticks to swimming.

She finds she can often get more done alone than in a team.

This means that she's **I**ntroverted but not very strongly. Being introverted doesn't mean she's a nerd or a social dead loss. It means she finds her energy and motivation from within. She can play at being an extrovert as much as she wants to, and enjoy it, but she wouldn't try to do it every day.

Detail or Big Picture

She loves to be creative. There's always some imaginary situation going on in her head. She is happier when working on a new program where she creates fresh material instead of trudging through theory. Sometimes she wishes she had chosen Art or French instead of computing for a degree.

When she programs, she loves to visualise the big picture in her mind and then to create the code. Checking every dot and comma is not so interesting for her. In fact she doesn't always do it very well.

She trusts her instinct. If something feels wrong then she avoids it. She doesn't always feel the need for a rational explanation.

That means she's a **B**ig picture person. She loves the future and new ideas. Today's details can be boring. Of all the descriptions of the personality traits, this one leaps out at her the most strongly. Reading the description, she's saying yes, yes, yes, that's me. Was there one of them that was the same for you?

Logical Thinker or Follow Your Heart

When there's a big decision to be made, she gets the pen and paper out and writes down all the pros and cons. She weighs it all up carefully, logically. She makes the decision first and looks at how it might affect other people second. If the issue is important, then it might be unavoidable to upset someone.

If someone's music is too loud then she asks him or her to turn it down. She's not terribly bothered if they think that's harsh.

So she's a **L**ogical Thinker. But it's not terribly strong – she can see the other point of view quite easily.

Structured or Free

This one is very difficult for her to decide. She can see herself clearly in both of the descriptions. She enjoys being free, but she knows that it doesn't get much done. If she got up from the laptop every time she felt like it, then she simply wouldn't get her work finished. She sets goals for herself, but includes free time in the plan towards each goal.

She chose not to make a decision between **S**tructured and F̲ree. She's a bit of both. And that's okay. You don't have to choose one side or the other just for the sake of it. You can sit right in the middle.

So, overall Nicola is:

- slightly **Introverted** rather than Extroverted
- strongly **Big Picture** rather than Detail
- more of a **Logical Thinker** than Follow Your Heart
- and right in the middle of **Free** or **Structured**.

Imagine her in a job where she was checking really fine detail all day long, not able to put in any ideas of her own and every time she found something wrong, her boss would get terribly upset and emotional. And on top of that, other people constantly interrupted her. She'd be miserable. She could do it for a while but it would not fit her at all. She wouldn't draw much satisfaction from it, she'd just grit her teeth and get on with it, hoping that the next task would be more fun.

Now imagine a job where she was required to come up with new ideas and think them through to see if they were workable. A job where she had a close relationship with a few co-workers, but wasn't being constantly interrupted. Can you see how that is much more likely to be a satisfying position for her?

Four different temperaments

There is another way to look at personality that can be a bit simpler to take on board. For thousands of years, philosophers and others have described four temperaments of humanity. These four temperaments have come up all the way from Hypocrites to the American Indian Medicine Wheel. The personality traits above can be combined to describe four different temperaments. It can be very useful to look at which one of the four you are. It will help confirm which of the traits best describe you and it helps a lot when identifying Job Activities for you.

Each of these temperaments is defined by a combination of two traits from the eight that we have been through. Each temperament has its own name, but you can remember them as the combination of the two traits if that's easier. Everyone fits into one of these temperaments, but again some more strongly than others.

Here are the four:

Idealists	**'Big Picture' and 'Follow Your Heart'**	**BH**
Theorists	**'Big Picture' and 'Logical Thinker'**	**BL**
Traditionalists	**'Detail' and 'Structured'**	**DS**
Live for the Moment	**'Detail' and 'Free'**	**DF**

Look at the descriptions below of the four temperaments. Read them all, and if the one that seems most like you doesn't match with the traits you chose earlier then go back and have a look at the traits again. (This is the sort of problem where a full-length personality test can help out).

Idealists – 'Big Picture' and 'Follow Your Heart' – BH

Idealists are good communicators, problem solvers and are interested in other people. They have strong personal values and are often religious or spiritually inclined. They love to help other people and to bring out the best in others. They like change and are particularly interested in how change affects the people involved in it. Idealists can be quite emotional and are not always terribly practical.

Idealists don't enjoy having to discipline others. They value authentic friends and colleagues. They prefer harmony to discourse.

Theorist – Big Picture and Logical Thinker – BL

Theorists love to plan and strategise. They can come up with complex theories and see relationships and connections between events and facts that others may miss. They have high intellectual standards and expect those around them to measure up to the same standards. They are naturally curious and like to learn. They love change and don't like to accept things as they are. They are full of vision and innovation. Theorists want to be good at what they do and can be very competitive.

Theorists can tend to make things a bit more complicated than necessary and can lose other people's interest along the way. They can be a little unaware of the effect that they have on others and so can sometimes be seen as arrogant and remote. Theorists can have trouble with authority – and specifically superiors they consider to be less intelligent or qualified than themselves. They can get bored with work that they don't feel is intellectually challenging.

Traditionalist – Detail and Structure – DS

Traditionalists love to belong to a structured organisation. They respect rules and are happy in a hierarchy. They are often quite conservative and they feel a duty to society and their company or organisation. They are responsible and like to 'do the right thing'. They respect law and order. They like to get things right first time. They work hard and value efficiency.

Traditionalists tend not to be big risk takers and don't like too much change. They like stability. They are not very keen on abstract ideas, they prefer the concrete, the here and now. It's possible that some may see them as inflexible and unimaginative.

Live for the Moment – Detail and Free – DF

Live for the Moment people like to enjoy each day as it comes. They like action and are happy to act on impulse. That doesn't mean they are necessarily frivolous or irresponsible, but they enjoy the freedom and spontaneity to seize the moment when it arrives. They are happy to take risks and look up to acts of heroism. They can be quite practical and are often good with their hands. They don't worry about tradition and don't like to follow rules. They can be really good in a crisis, being able to pick up the facts fast and offer practical solutions.

Live for the Moment people can have problems with authority and can be seen as unpredictable by some. They can get bored with repetitive tasks and work that has a slow steady pace. They don't mind living life near the edge sometimes.

Which of the four temperaments seems most like you? Did it confirm the traits you had already chosen?

I would describe myself as a ________________.

Chapter three summary

☑ **Each of us is different and wonderfully unique, but our personalities do follow patterns. You want to predict which job will be right and you can use these patterns of personality to help you do that.**

☑ **The chapter should have given you some insight into personality traits and how they describe you.**

☑ **Have another look through the descriptions if you're not sure you relate to it all yet. It can be easier to form a first idea, take a break and then have another look at it. There's no hurry.**

☑ **It's good to do a full test with an expert, especially if you had trouble identifying yourself with the descriptions of the personality traits.**

Next ➔➔

Next we look at how personality information can suggest Job Activities for you.

4

Your Job Activities List

Now that you've had a go at finding activities that you are good at and like on your own and we have been through some personality theory, we're going to combine the temperaments and personality traits with Job Activities.

Here's a list of common Job Activities. Beside most of the activities we have included the temperament and/or personality trait that usually goes best with that particular activity. Bear in mind that matching activities and personality is not an exact science, especially as we only gave an introduction to personality here in the book rather than a full test and explanation. Use the personality information as a guide to help your thinking, and not as a set of definite rules. If the personality trait and temperament information points you to an activity that you feel is not right for you, then don't choose it for your list.

The temperament and trait column is left blank for some activities. In these cases it is not very reliable to guide people of a certain personality towards the activity – it could be suitable for anyone depending on other the factors.

Go through activities on the list that fit you. Most people find it easier to go down each column one by one, so (a) go through the personality and temperament column, then (b) tick what you like, (c) what you are good at and finally (d) tick activities that match your previous experience.

So, get ticking over the next five pages.

Job activity	Suggested suitable tempera-ment or trait	JAs you like	JAs you are good at	JAs from exper-ience
Serving customers	Idealist Extravert			
Teaching (enjoying the people)	Idealist Extravert			
Communicating with people	Idealist			
Understanding others	Idealist			
Working with warm relationships	Idealist			
Being appreciated by others	Idealist			
Working in groups	Idealist			
Caring for other people	Idealist			
Helping people	Idealist			
Work involving sympathy and empathy	Idealist			
Working for the good of others	Idealist			
Presenting to people	Idealist			
Public speaking	Idealist			
Working in a stress-free environment	Idealist, Live the moment			
Work that involves physical action	Live the moment			

Job activity	Suggested suitable tempera-ment or trait	JAs you like	JAs you are good at	JAs from exper-ience
Getting up and moving around - local travel	Live the moment			
Being flexible	Live the moment			
Dealing with a crisis	Live the moment			
Producing physical products	Live the moment			
Selling products or services	Live the moment			
International travelling	Live the moment			
Repairing physical things	Live the moment			
Work involving adventure	Live the moment			
Work that is fast and furious	Live the moment			
Working under pressure	Live the moment			
Setting your own work plan	Theorist, Live moment			
Competing with others	Theorist			
Learning new skills and concepts	Theorist			
Teaching complex material	Theorist			
Going it alone	Theorist			

Job activity	Suggested suitable tempera-ment or trait	JAs you like	JAs you are good at	JAs from exper-ience
Using imagination	Theorist, Idealist			
Work that involves changing things	Theorist			
Creating new ideas	Theorist, Idealist			
Creative writing	Theorist, Idealist			
Creative design	Traditionalist			
Having high responsibilities	Traditionalist			
Being respected by others	Traditionalist			
Belonging to an organisation	Traditionalist			
Checking for mistakes	Traditionalist			
Being in a secure position	Traditionalist			
Following tradition	Traditionalist			
Working to deadlines	Traditionalist			
Using defined skills learned in training	Traditionalist			
Working to existing procedures	Traditionalist			
Following instructions	Traditionalist			

Job activity	Suggested suitable tempera-ment or trait	JAs you like	JAs you are good at	JAs from exper-ience
Factual writing	Traditionalist Live moment			
Designing to established procedures	Traditionalist Live moment			
Making decisions	Traditionalist Theorist			
Managing people	Traditionalist Theorist			
Instructing people	Traditionalist Theorist			
Performing numerical calculations				
Using different languages				
Working with words				
Researching				
Investigating into facts				
Working in teams				
Participating in meetings				
Working with computers and IT				
Being in the office				
Multi-tasking - doing many tasks at the same time	Extrovert			

Job activity	Suggested suitable tempera-ment or trait	JAs you like	JAs you are good at	JAs from exper-ience
Single-tasking, doing one task at a time	Introvert			
Studying and sitting exams				
Computer programming	Detail people			
Science-based work				
General use of the PC				
Supporting and assisting				
Editing others' work				
Proof reading	Traditionalist Introvert			
Disciplining people with rules	Logical thinker			
Translating	Introvert			
Working with overseas cultures				

Now let's get all the JAs you have identified together and choose the best five for you. Look across the rows and see if you have any JAs with three or four ticks. They are the ones that probably suit you the best. Then have a look for JAs with one or two ticks in the row.

JAs from the table with *three or four ticks* are:

JAs with *one or two ticks* are:

Now take a moment to consider these activities. Do they look right to you? Use your judgement as well as following the ticks. If there's an activity there that does not appeal to you then cross it out, or if there's one in the list that does appeal to you, feel free to add it. You need to feel good about these activities.

Now pick five JAs from the table above that *appeal* the most:

And write down the rest of the activities on your list in the spaces below. These are your supporting activities.

Well done. That's your Job Activity list. When you are reading company brochures or job descriptions and even job adverts, have this list with you. Look for matches. You probably will not get an exact match in any job description but you can get a good amount of overlap. When you do get a good overlap, you will know that the day-to-day activities of that job are a good fit for you.

Next ➔➔

Let's move on to the next chapter where we really get down to the crunch. How to look at jobs.

5

Introduction to jobs

Introduction

Let's have another look at the career decisions model.

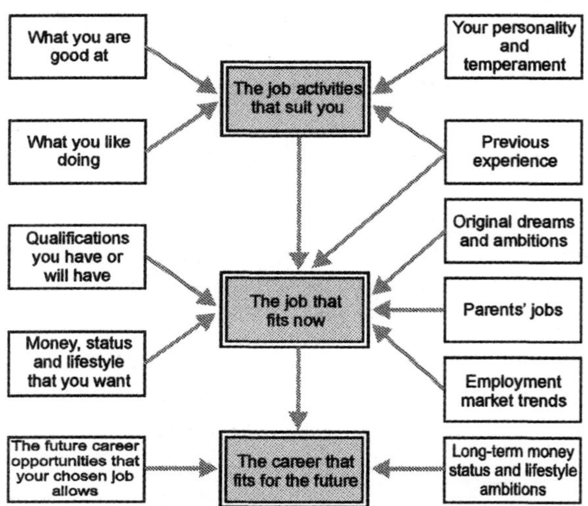

We have finished the top box, your Job Activities and now we're looking at the middle one, Jobs. There's a quick introduction then we go on to the sections of the model that feed the job decision in the next few chapters.

How to start thinking about the jobs

There's one main reason we go to work. It's **money**.

Everybody needs some. People don't get up at 6 o'clock every morning because they like the office wallpaper. But money should never be the only consideration in a career choice – it's one factor that goes into your decision.

When you're choosing a job, make sure you really understand what it's all about. We have said it before and we'll probably say it again. Understand it from every perspective possible. Get to know the job as well as you can. Talk to people who do it or have done it. Read about it. Talk to your friends about it. Understand where the job will take you in the future as well as what it's like now.

Most people don't do this well enough. It's hard to get underneath the skin of a company or an industry until you are employed in it. But it's not impossible. Summer jobs and work shadowing are both good ways to have a look for yourself.

Reading company brochures gives you a limited picture. They only tell you what they think will bring in the best recruits, or sell the most products.

Here is an example from my own career. I graduated with a BA and Masters in Chemical Engineering and took a job in the USA as a design engineer for a firm that built chemical plants. (Petrol additives plants and oil refineries).

I thought the job would be very creative, full of problem solving and other intellectually stimulating challenges. Design work is in teams so I thought that there would be a great deal of team interaction and a good working spirit within the company.

Well, some of that was true, but there were a few things that I had not thought of. A chemical plant is built from hundreds of thousands of parts. Engineers have to make lists of every part, and run calculations to specify them. Once you have specified one pipe or relief valve, the rest are more or less the same. The first few are interesting, the tenth is okay, but the seven-hundred-and-twenty-third is not exactly a journey into new conceptual territory. And then someone else has to check every single calculation. Some of the older engineers had been doing this for twenty years and they were quite dispirited and cynical.

My first job as a chemical design engineer was not a bad job overall, the hours were reasonable, I travelled to lots of interesting places and the money was very good for a fresh graduate, but it wasn't a very good fit for me.

The nature of what I was doing day-to-day was completely different from what I had expected and had done at college, even though it was the job that naturally followed my degree. To be honest, I found most of the days there a bit boring and unchallenging. The job didn't suit me very well. I remember one day checking my watch at 7:15 in the morning – only 525 minutes to go!

I was 23, straight out of college and single, but the people in the firm were almost all over 35, married and although they were mostly pleasant professionally, they were not very interested in socialising after work.

I prefer uncertainty and challenge in life than predictability and safety. If I had spent time to look objectively at myself and if I had known exactly what the job entailed on a day-to-day basis, I would probably not have taken it. Think back to the four temperaments, I was a 23-year-old Theorist in a 50-year-old Traditionalist's job.

You can avoid that kind of mistake – read on.

Next ➔➔

We're going to have a look at each section of the Career Decisions Model that feeds into the job decision:

- **your original dreams or ambitions**
- **parents' occupation and opinions**
- **people with whom you work**
- **qualifications**
- **previous work experience**
- **trends in the employment market**
- **future career opportunities, money and lifestyle.**

6

Original Dreams or Ambitions

Most of us have, or had a dream of who we wanted to be or what we wanted to do. For some people the dream was realistic and attainable. Great – think it through with all the information we talk about in the Career Decisions Model and if it still fits then go ahead and do it.

However a lot of us have dreams that are not very realistic. Not everyone can become a famous actor or a Prime Minister. But you can still learn from your original ambitions.

Let's take a really unrealistic dream. Melissa wanted to be a Princess. That's a tough dream, you're either born a Princess or once a generation one girl in the country marries a Prince. Melissa's lovely, but just in terms of probability we can be more or less certain she won't become a Princess. But what she can do is ask herself why she wanted to be a Princess? What did she perceive that a Princess does or has that is attractive to her?

Well, a Princess has money, status, lots of appreciation from people around her and beautiful clothes. If Melissa dreamed of being a Princess then she wants to be appreciated, be elegant, well dressed and rich. This isn't fantasy anymore, these are helpful hints for her in searching for a career that fits. She could draw out some Job Activities from this dream. Being appreciated – so she needs to work in a prominent position that involves a lot of other people. Being rich – the hard hours of a high paying job could well be worth the effort for Melissa. Beautiful clothes – aesthetic appeal is important to her. She's more likely to be happy working in advertising in the fashion industry than heavy maintenance in the oil industry. Can you see how we've moved from unrealistic fantasy to helpful information here?

Let's look at another common example. Brian wanted to be an astronaut. A bit more chance of getting there than becoming a Prince, but not that much, especially if you live in the UK, as we don't actually have any space shuttles. What did Brian think an astronaut does? An astronaut explores, takes risks, deals with the highest technology available, and he or she can go it alone, but is possibly not rich.

So Brian might have quite a high preference for risk and be technically oriented. If he dreamed about being alone for weeks in a hi-tech baked bean tin thousands of miles from earth, then he is probably quite independent. Perhaps he could be happy and successful as an entrepreneur in a technical field.

That's a big leap to make – astronaut to entrepreneur – it's just an example and there are a lot of steps missing from an informed career decision, but you can see how going back to your early thoughts or dreams can actually be helpful. It can identify some Job Activities that you will enjoy.

Have a think about it for yourself.

When I was younger, I dreamed of being a: (write it down – even if it seems really silly. You can scrub it out before anyone else sees!)

The sorts of things a ____________________ does are:

You should now have some reasonably helpful notes – perhaps not to be taken too literally, but it's another slice of the pie, another source of information for you to consider before you make the big decision.

Chapter six summary

- ☑ **If you have always had a dream that is quite practical in terms of employment, then it really could be a good career for you, but don't follow it blindly.**
- ☑ **Go through the whole process we have outlined and check that it does actually fit you.**
- ☑ **If you have a dream that is not very realistic, don't ignore it. There is useful information waiting for you.**
- ☑ **Look for similarities between your dream and the real world.**
- ☑ **Use Job Activities as the go between.**

Next ➔➔

Let's think about your background and what your parents do.

7

Parents' Occupation and Opinions

Fifty years ago, it was quite normal for sons to follow in their fathers' footsteps and for daughters to get married and become housewives. The entire shape of industry and employment has changed since then and it's changing faster and faster every year. Most notably, it's now just as common for daughters to go out and get great jobs as it is for sons.

However, social expectations change more slowly than the shape of the employment market. There is still often a pressure or an expectation to do what your parents did, or at least to choose an area that has the same social acceptability. There may be a family expectation to stay in the same geographical area as well. A farmer's son won't get any raised eyebrows for going to college to study agriculture, but he might have a difficult time persuading his hard working folks to fund a degree in Ancient Chinese Theology.

There are many possible advantages and disadvantages to following what your parents do or did. Learn as much as you can from them, and then look at their jobs objectively to see if the same career would suit you. Don't follow any single source of advice blindly whether it's your parents, a personality test or anything else. Put it into perspective with all the other factors that we show you in the Career Decision Model.

Advantages of following in your folks' footsteps:

- You will have heard about their jobs from an early age and so you probably know more about them than any others. If you can remain objective, then this information gives you a real advantage in being able to judge whether it is the right career for you. The familiarity and inside information you have can reduce the risk that you misjudge a career by only seeing it from the outside.

- You can do almost all of your job research sitting at the kitchen table, and it's first hand information not advertising or recruitment blurb.

- You have a ready network of job contacts waiting for you. If you have decided for yourself that this is the career that you want then you should use these contacts – most people aren't that lucky.

Disadvantages of following in your folks' footsteps:

- As we have already said, the right job for you is all about fit. And you are not a clone copy of one of your parents – you're a unique individual. Your desires and dreams may be completely different, your personality and temperament may be completely different. (Personality type is not handed down from one generation to the next). Your ambitions may be different. The same job simply might not fit.

- It is possible that your folks themselves are not actually very well suited to their jobs. They probably didn't look at the big picture or use a career decision model when they chose their careers – these sorts of methods were not readily available then, and it used to be much more difficult to change career even just twenty years ago. People tended to stay with the same firm for a long time and almost always in the same industry.

- The job your parent(s) did might have been attractive when they started out but might not be very attractive now. For example the oil industry in the sixties and seventies was enjoying a massive boom. Many countries were building from scratch on huge new oil fields. Oil workers could make fortunes by going out to the

Middle East for a few years. Now however there is nothing like as much growth, it's a much less attractive market to work in than it used to be.

Listen with an open mind to what they do but don't feel under pressure to follow, even if they expect you to. Social pressure can be very strong, but it's often not very good career advice. There are advantages there for you if one of your parent's careers does suit you, but look at all the other factors that go into the decision to make sure it does fit, otherwise you could be in for a big disappointment.

Chapter seven summary

☑ **Look at what your folks do, but look at it as one source of information among many.**

☑ **Even if you are set on 'doing what your old man did' go through the whole process of selecting your Job Activities and matching them to jobs.**

☑ **Find out whether the job fits before you get there, not three years afterwards.**

Next ➔➔

We will look at a surprisingly important point in deciding about a job.

8

People with Whom You Work

The people around you at work make a huge difference to whether you enjoy yourself. They can also help you to succeed or ensure that you don't. Of all the issues to try to predict when you are choosing a career, the people with whom you will work is the hardest. There is simply no way of knowing for sure who will be sitting at the next desk in four year's time. But there are trends, cultures, age distributions and gravitations of one social group or another towards particular careers, and it's all worth thinking about.

Here are a couple of examples to show you what we mean.

1 – A traditional industry dominated by forty- to sixty-five year-old men

Imagine you've just left college and you get your first job. You join the marketing department of a firm that trades big volumes of building materials. It's big business and there is money to be made, but it is very well established, it's not changing fast. At best it's a steady market. Chances are that it will be dominated by forty- to sixty-five year-old men. A lot of traditional industries still are. And you come in bright eyed and bushy tailed at twenty-three.

Now you have been there three years and you've been working hard. You have nice colleagues there, but outside work you don't see much of them. You're out razzing it up on a Saturday night and they're putting their slippers on and lighting up another pipe.

You want responsibility, you want important work, you want progression and pay rises. To progress, you will have to persuade your fifty-five year-old boss that you know more about the business than the next guy. Here's the problem, he's forty-five, he's been doing the job for twenty years and for fifteen of them he's been playing golf with your boss every Sunday. And while they're playing golf, their wives are playing bridge and planning the latest community help project that the local church is going to start.

Is he going to promote you? The answer is almost certainly not. And how good you are at the job probably won't even enter into the decision. You're viewed as the kid, the young thing that needs another fifteen years at least to mature into anything worthwhile. The defining factor in your career is not you or your performance, it's the age of the people around you. And that can be very bad news. They have to retire or cock their toes early for you to get a chance to progress. If you want a steady nine-to-fiver without much responsibility or progression then it might be okay. Not everyone wants the competition and stress of a fast moving work environment. But if you have career goals, you will probably spend more time dreaming about them than achieving them, and it's solely because of the age structure of the employees in the company.

2 – A new technology business full of bright young to middle-aged people

Now imagine you join a small IT firm. The Managing Director is forty-two; the Head of Operations is thirty-five. They provide cutting edge IT solutions and there are almost as many women as men. A product that is two years old is a dinosaur to them. You do your first few years learning the shape of the business and working hard on some projects. You work alongside people like you and you make good friends.

They're about to bring out a new product and they need people to implement it in their clients' offices. Because the product is new, only a very few people know how to implement it – obvious eh? They have to train some more people and they choose you. You do well in the training. You do one project under someone else's guidance, it goes well and they ask you to lead a small project. You are now a hot potato at twenty-six. Go out there and get cooking. If you continue to perform, you could be managing large complex projects at the age of thirty and taking home serious money. There is no one who has been doing the job for twenty years because the product has only existed for six months. Your future is in your hands. If you perform, you get rewarded. No one has to retire or have a heart attack for you to have a chance to progress. If you want a quiet, stress-free life then it might not be the best fit for you, but if you are ambitious, if you want responsibility and progression, then this type of young fast moving company is much more likely to give you what you want.

When you look at a job or a career, try to find out the following points about the people who work there.

- Age structure – how do you fit into it?
- General level of qualification in the employees – how do you compare?
- Is it male dominated? – does that matter to you?
- Does it consist of people from a particular social background, and again, does that matter to you?
- Is it an international community or not?

Chapter eight summary

☑ **You can't predict whether your co-workers in any particular career will be nice or not, but you probably can predict how old and how qualified they will be. That can make a huge difference to your career.**

Next ➔➔

We will look into qualifications and how they affect you.

9

Qualifications

Qualifications open the front door of companies. They get you into the interview room. They don't automatically get you the job and there's a lot more to being successful than having qualifications, but without them, the doors can all be closed.

If you are still at school, our very strong advice is for you to go to university or other higher education if you possibly can. If you are worrying about university debt – don't. The money you might have to borrow is nothing compared to the extra cash you will earn through the years with a degree or other higher education qualification. Higher education opens doors – without it you can be left standing outside on the pavement while everyone else walks in.

The rest of the chapter on qualifications is split for two different categories of reader.

- **Part 9A** for those still at school and wondering what to do later, and those of you considering going back into education to retrain for a new career;

- **Part 9B** for those of you who are going to stick with the qualifications you already have.

9A – You are still in education or about to go back into it

As we just said, you will always be better off having higher education qualifications. There used to be quite a few attractive jobs available to school leavers but they are becoming fewer and fewer. High street banks and insurance companies used to take on a large number of school leavers and provide all the necessary training, but now they look much more towards universities for their recruits. They still take school leavers, but the best opportunities in these firms now go to the graduates.

So let's assume you are at least seriously thinking about university or college. The next question is what to study.

If you have already chosen your career, then the choice of course is obviously much easier. If your career requires a particular course then the decision is already taken.

If your chosen career does not require a particular course, then try to choose something that you will do well in and keeps your options open. The same goes for people who want to wait until later to make their career choices.

If you are likely to get into one of the top universities (top ten or fifteen in the UK) and you expect to work hard there and do well (2.1 or 1st class honours), then you should be fine whatever you study. There are many jobs open to top graduates whatever their subject.

But be realistic. If you are not looking at a top ranked university and/or you think you might want to enjoy yourself quite a bit and risk lower grades, then you need to choose your course carefully. Most of the professional world is not waiting to embrace 2.2 or third class philosophy or ancient Greek students from educational establishments that they have never heard of. That doesn't mean you have to get into Oxford to get a decent job – not at all. You can get a great job with a solid degree from a lesser known university if it is relevant to the company you're interested in and if they like you, and once you are in, it doesn't matter where you came from.

If you're not looking at a big name university, then we suggest you choose a subject that is directly career related. Of course that means that you need to have a reasonable idea about your future career as well. That might be tough to accept when we're saying people who go to Oxbridge can study whatever they fancy and you have to get your hands dirty with a topic that might a bit more hard work, but it's reality. You can still end up in a position that's really great for you later on but you need to be a little bit more focussed on how you get there.

That was the reality for me when I wanted to change my career from engineering to management consultancy. I had a very good CV but the fact was that the names of the companies I had worked for were not quite well enough respected to launch me straight into consultancy. I had to do an MBA. It was a year of incredibly hard work, studying from 9 am until 10 pm six days a week, sometimes seven. It wasn't much fun and it cost me twenty five thousand quid – every single penny I had saved since starting work, but it got me where I wanted to go.

There is a table of university courses and the jobs that follow on from them at the end of this chapter. There's also a list of jobs that don't require a specific university degree. Browse through them to help you think about which course is best for you.

If you still don't have any idea what to study, here are a couple of suggestions. These are hints for the few of you who are a bit lost and were about to pick a subject out of the hat – it's not supposed to be general advice for all potential students.

- If you are **more technically based** (you liked maths, physics, chemistry at school) think about Computer Sciences or Electronic Engineering. If you like a mix of technical and non-technical then economics can be a good bet. The courses for these subjects are generally very rigorous and companies regard them highly. You get all the logical problem-solving training that the pure science degrees give but it's all in a real world context.

- If you were **more arts or language based** think about a modern language. Language is fundamental to everything we do and employers who are not looking for numerical or technical skills will look for graduates with a solid command of language and communication. The business world is so international now that employees who are fluent in a second and even third language have a real advantage.

9B – Advice for those of you who have decided to stick with the qualifications that you already have

The first question is obvious – will the qualifications that you already have get you into the interview room for the job you want? If the answer is yes, then great, move onto the next section of the book. If not then you still have some options:

- You can try for the job anyway – we have some techniques to help you.
- You can choose another job in the same firm that is close to the one you really want and move sideways after a period of time.
- Or you can decide to retrain after all (possibly the best bet).

Trying for the job anyway

It is possible to land jobs when you are under-qualified on paper, but it's definitely an uphill struggle. If you don't have a thick skin, then think twice before you start. The people who succeed almost always have something else up their sleeve that the company wants badly enough to waive the qualification requirement.

What do you have up you sleeve? Don't say 'your elbow'. All right, say your elbow, but what else? And how can you present it so that someone will pick it up on your CV in around ten seconds? That's how long it takes a recruitment professional to check a CV for appropriate qualifications and bin it if the right letters aren't there.

Here are some of the sorts of things that can get you around a lack of qualifications.

- You know someone in the firm and they like you.
- You have exceptional experience and you can make a great story out of it.
- You have a fluent language or some other unusual skill that the company needs and can't find in a fully qualified applicant.

Here are some points that probably will not get you around a lack of qualifications.

- I'm really keen and I'm sure I could do it if they'd just give me the chance.
- I started the course for the qualification, but I didn't finish it.

Make a really interesting story of whatever it is that you have to offer. Read the second part of this book, where we talk at length about how to put stories of your experience together. Go through the process, write out your story to see if you have a realistic chance of getting the job. Bring out facts, results, evidence and numbers. Then look at it as objectively as you can. Get someone else to look at it as well if possible. Ask yourself the question, if I was an interviewer would I think that this story is as valuable to the company as the qualification that you are missing? And lastly make sure that your story or skill leaps out of your CV and is in the first sentence of your covering letter – otherwise you may never get the chance to tell them about it.

My publisher tells of the time many years ago when he applied for a job which had two 'essentials' in its person specification – qualifications and experience in training and qualifications and experience in social work. He had plenty of the first but none of the second. However, he made much play of his several years' experience as a London policeman and got the job. The employers found that an acceptable alternative to their original wishes.

Moving sideways

Another option is to take a job that you can get with your qualifications that has contact with people in the job that you really want. If you do well and get to know the right people, you may have a chance to move sideways into the position.

A friend of mine wanted to get into the change management section of the firm I used to work for, but he had no experience or training in change management. He was in the project management department. He read up about change management a great deal and knew the subject, but that wasn't enough to get him a transfer. He waited until he was working on a job that involved both change management and project management and went for the sideways move. He worked incredible hours to help the change management team as much as he could and still do all of his own work. They recognised his effort and ability and offered him a transfer. But it took time and very hard work, and there's no guarantee that you will be able to make the leap. Moving sideways is a game of politics and snakes and ladders. Make sure you are at least reasonably satisfied with the job you take to position yourself for the move – you might be stuck with it for quite a while.

Chapter nine summary

☑ **You're better of with higher education than without it, and don't worry about debt. You will pay it off.**

☑ **If you're under-qualified for the job you want, there may be ways round the problem, but re-training could still be your best bet.**

☑ **Choice of degree subjects: a good degree in any subject (2.1 or 1st) from a famous university should position you well for employment.**

☑ **Landing your ideal job coming from a lesser-known university with a non-vocational degree can be harder.**

☑ **The same applies if you get very bad grades. If you think you may be in this category, then go for a career related subject in a growing market sector – you have much more chance of getting relevant employment afterwards.**

Courses and careers lists

Very many graduate jobs do not need a specific degree. Here is a list of typical examples of these jobs.

Insurance industry
Marketing
Advertising
Law (via 2 years in law school)
Banking (easier to get in with a numerical/technical background)
Accountancy (easier to get in with a numerical/technical background)
Stock broking (easier to get in with a numerical/technical background)
Investment fund management (easier to get in with a numerical/technical background)
IT Consultancy (easier to get in with a numerical/technical background)
Human resources
Public Relations
Police & Customs
Armed Forces (officer training)
Social work
Civil Service and Politics
Leisure industry and sports management
Teaching (via teacher training)
Recruitment consultancy
Property industry
Media
Journalism

Now here's a table of examples of jobs that follow a particular degree. If you want further information on courses and the jobs that they can lead to have a look at **www.prospects.ac.uk**.

Accountancy	Accountancy, company finance, auditing, tax advice, Inland Revenue, treasury, merchant banking, general business management, corporate finance, management consultancy

Art	Art and antiques industry, auctioneering
Architecture	Architecture, project management, town planning, industrial design, landscape architecture
Biology	Conservation, academic research, industrial research, lab technician
Bio-chemistry	Research, clinical biochemistry, forensic science
Classics & Ancient Languages	Writing, publishing
Chemistry	Chemical research (academic and industrial), chemicals production and quality assurance, pharmaceuticals
Economics	Economist, accountancy, banking, management consultancy, insurance, actuary
Engineering – Mechanical	Manufacturing and mechanical design, production management, factory design and construction. Project management
Engineering – Chemical	Oil and chemicals production, and plant design. Project management, pharmaceuticals
Engineering – Electrical	Electricity production and equipment design. Network design and operation
Engineering – Aero	Aeronautical engineer (design and manufacture), project management, air safety
Engineering – Mining	Mining operations engineer, mining equipment design and production, project management

Engineering – Marine	Marine architecture, shipping industry, insurance, project management
Engineering – Civil	Civil engineering (buildings, roads, bridges etc), town planning, surveying, project management
English	Publishing, law (via law school), writing, journalism, TV and Radio
Geography	Environmental consultancy, cartographer, town planning, logistics management
History	Historian, museum curator, archaeologist, archivist, genealogist
Law	Solicitor, barrister, judge, company lawyer, crown prosecutor
Maths	Accountancy, actuary, banking
Medicine	Doctor, surgeon, health management, medical supplies industry
Modern Languages	Translation, literature, publishing
Physics	Research (academic and industrial), medical physics, nuclear physics, meteorology, electronics and IT industries
Psychology	Clinical, occupational and educational psychology, counselling, social work and social research
Politics	Politician, civil service, political consultancy, public affairs, journalism, public relations
Veterinary science	Veterinary practice, animal pharmaceuticals, research

10

Previous Work Experience

We have already looked at your experience briefly in choosing your Job Activities.

Did you enjoy your experience and do you feel that it is a good fit for you in the future? If you didn't enjoy it, don't be afraid to say that you didn't like it and you don't want to carry on in that line of work. If you didn't like it then, it probably didn't fit.

That's an easier decision for a second-year student at university than for a middle-aged professional with a family and a mortgage, but the principle is the same, and many people do successfully change their jobs and even their whole careers these days. The time when most employees stayed with the same firm for 25 years is in the past.

To use your previous experience to the best advantage, think about transferable skills. These are the skills you developed or used in one job that are useful to another. We split them into two categories, direct and indirect.

Directly transferable skills are obviously relevant to the core of the new job you are looking at. An example could be financial modelling. If you have good financial modelling experience from project evaluation in an industrial company, you could use the exact same skill in a corporate finance department of a bank. It's directly relevant and makes you immediately attractive as a candidate. Generally, staying with directly transferable skills allows you to change jobs but not to change career. But there are many jobs in any career line and it is often possible to find a position with a reasonably different set of Job Activities using some of the same core skills. And that can be the difference between being happy and being miserable at work. Here's an example.

A friend of mine was a civil engineer; he started out doing reinforced concrete design. His skill was technical design knowledge, and his main activity was number crunching. Very solid stuff and not exiting enough for him. He moved to a risk assessment firm. They assess risk of construction projects. He still uses the same core skill, his technical knowledge of reinforced concrete design, but he has completely different activities. His job is now about assessing what other people have designed. He travels a lot more, he spends a day dealing with the numbers on a design rather than three weeks, and then he discusses opinions and options with the clients and the insurers. His activities are much more varied, faster paced and more people oriented. He's much happier in the role. He kept his directly transferable skill but changed his activities to suit him.

Indirectly transferable skills are areas that will be relevant to the prospective new job but will need to be re-packaged to be used effectively. An example could be modelling complex mechanical systems compared with financial modelling. The underlying skill is the same – manipulating a complex set of numbers and constraints in a spreadsheet to achieve an objective while complying with a particular set of rules. But the rules have changed. Mechanical models use the rules Isaac Newton came up with and financial models use the UK Accounting Standards. This example would require retraining, but others don't. Organising people is a classic transferable skill that has been the basis of many career changes.

Look at your transferable skills. How many are direct between the job(s) you have done and the new position that you are interested in and how many are indirect? Do the indirect ones require formal retraining to be useful in the new job?

In general, the more directly transferable your skills are, the easier it will be to make the leap. But plenty of people do change solely on indirect skills and possibly some training. Go through the second section of the book and look at experience stories. We show you how to present your experience in the most relevant way possible to the prospective job. When you research the new position and create your experience stories, you should start to have a feel for whether there really is much common ground between your experience and the new position.

Chapter ten summary

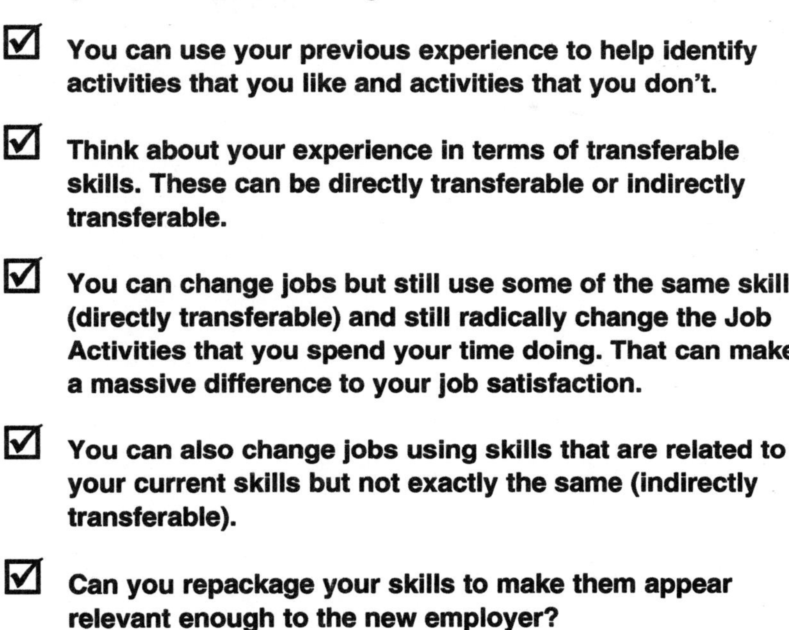

☑ You can use your previous experience to help identify activities that you like and activities that you don't.

☑ Think about your experience in terms of transferable skills. These can be directly transferable or indirectly transferable.

☑ You can change jobs but still use some of the same skills (directly transferable) and still radically change the Job Activities that you spend your time doing. That can make a massive difference to your job satisfaction.

☑ You can also change jobs using skills that are related to your current skills but not exactly the same (indirectly transferable).

☑ Can you repackage your skills to make them appear relevant enough to the new employer?

☑ The technique of experience stories in section two of the book will help you to do it.

Next ➔➔

Now you have a better idea of what you want, let's see how it fits with trends in the employment market.

11

Trends in the Employment Market

Changes in the employment market have a big effect on career decisions. If you join a buoyant, growing sector, you can be swept along by a surge of demand for your services. When you're in demand you get good training, you get good pay rises and you have a world of opportunity ahead of you.

If you're in a shrinking market, there are more people than jobs. It's dog eat dog, and there are lots of dogs. People are retraining like mad and the employment market is flooded with ex-whatever's trying to re-create themselves.

If you are open to suggestions, then look for the growing markets. If all the influences on your decision point towards a steady market then go for it. But beware the shrinking market. You need really serious reasons to enter one – like your family has a business there or something like that. Even then the first thing you should think about is to diversify into another market.

The place to find the most up to date growth figures is the Internet. There is an excellent site called SKILLSBASE – labour market information database. (By the Department for Education and Skills and Warwick Institute for Employment Research). It provides a wide range of information and data on employment and skills. Below are the addresses of the homepage, and the page that gets you directly to the job-by-job growth projections.

Homepage
http://skillsbase.dfes.gov.uk/Narrative/Narrative.asp?sect=5

Job projections
http://skillsbase.dfes.gov.uk/Narrative/Narrative.asp?sect=5&page=7

Look through tables 1 and 2 on the following pages. Table 1 is a summary of 25 job categories with figures for the projected growth up to 2010. Also included are the replacement demands of each category and supporting data such as the total number of jobs in each category and the percentage of each category in the employment market. Replacement demands are the number of positions coming open due to people leaving the category because of retirement, moving to other industries, relocation and mortality. Table 2 expands the 25 categories into 81 more detailed professions so you can look specifically for the professions that interest you.

The tables show that business professionals (lawyers, accountants etc) are projected to see strong growth, along with science and technology, health industry and leisure and sports industries. Within science and technology information and communication professionals are projected to see the largest growth. Agriculture, skilled manual trades, plant operators, and basic clerical workers are all projected to see strong decline.

Bear in mind when you look at these data that the employment market can be quite volatile and the growth or decline of any particular industry can change year to year. This is a ten-year forecast. It did not predict, for example the short-term decline in communications technology shortly after the millennium. Use these figures as a guide but try to look for more detailed and up to date information when you choose your job. The Economist and business newspapers will provide a more immediate picture.

Employment growth and replacement projections.

Table 1

					1999		2010			
		GROWTH (Percentage change in number of jobs for the category)	New positions as a percentage of total jobs for the category (growth plus replacement demand)	New positions opening up per year (Actual change plus replacement demand)	Number of jobs	% of total	Number of jobs	% of total	Actual change in number of jobs	Replacement Demand
		Percent over 10 yr period	Percent over 10 yr period	(thousands of jobs)	(thousands of jobs)	Percent	(thousands of jobs)	Percent	(thousands of jobs)	(thousands of jobs)
	EMPLOYMENT CATEGORY									
1	**Corporate Managers**	**8.3**	**22.7**	657	2669	9.7	2891	9.7	222	435
2	**Managers and Proprietors in Agriculture and services**	**-15.4**	**60.2**	498	978	3.5	827	2.8	-151	649
3	**Science / Tech Professionals**	**28.2**	**48.1**	552	895	3.2	1147	3.9	252	300
4	**Health Professionals**	**38.9**	**58.7**	199	244	0.9	339	1.1	95	104
5	**Teaching / Research professionals**	**21.3**	**56.1**	821	1206	4.4	1463	4.9	257	564
6	**Business / Public Service Prof.**	**36.7**	**43.6**	423	710	2.6	971	3.3	261	162
7	**Science Associate Professionals**	**0.3**	**35.3**	142	401	1.5	402	1.4	1	140
8	**Health Associate Professionals**	**25**	**49.4**	546	884	3.2	1105	3.7	221	325
9	**Protective Service Occupations**	**20.3**	**27.3**	88	268	1	322	1.1	54	33
10	**Culture / Media / Sport Occupations**	**29.9**	**63.2**	408	498	1.8	646	2.2	149	259
11	**Business /Public Service Associate Professionals**	**26.1**	**45.0**	791	1393	5.1	1756	5.9	363	428
12	**Admin & clerical Occupations**	**5.5**	**43.7**	1338	2905	10.5	3065	10.3	160	1178
13	**Secretarial & Related Occupations**	**-9.1**	**40.7**	422	1141	4.1	1038	3.5	-104	526
14	**Skilled Agricultural Trades**	**-11.7**	**39.7**	115	328	1.2	290	1	-39	154
15	**Skilled Metal / Electrical Trades**	**-7.4**	**31.6**	452	1545	5.6	1432	4.8	-114	565
16	**Skilled Construction and Building Trades**	**-6.5**	**34.6**	324	1001	3.6	936	3.2	-65	389
17	**Textiles. Printing and Other Skilled Trades**	**2.3**	**49.2**	456	905	3.3	926	3.1	21	435
18	**Caring Personal Service Occupations**	**45.5**	**76.0**	1144	1034	3.8	1505	5.1	471	673
19	**Leisure / Other Personal Service Occupations**	**31.1**	**64.6**	475	560	2	735	2.5	174	301
20	**Sales Occupations**	**10.1**	**58.9**	1111	1714	6.2	1886	6.4	172	939
21	**Customer Service Occupations**	**5.6**	**45.8**	49	101	0.4	107	0.4	6	43
22	**Process, Plant & Machine Operators**	**-8.4**	**33.1**	455	1499	5.4	1373	4.6	-126	581
23	**Transport Drivers and Operators**	**2.4**	**43.9**	425	947	3.4	969	3.3	23	402
24	**Elementary Occupations: Trades, Plant and Machine Related**	**-2.2**	**45.5**	458	1030	3.7	1007	3.4	-23	481
25	**Elementary Occupations: Clerical / Service Related**	**-5.7**	**46.2**	1172	2690	9.8	2535	8.5	-154	1327
	All occupations	**7.7**		13522	27546	100	29673	100	2127	11395

Source: Warwick Institute for Employment Research, Projections of Occupations and Qualifications, 2000/2001, Tables 4.4 and 4.5

	Detailed employment growth projections				
	Table 2				
		1999	2010		
		Number of jobs (thousands)	Number of jobs (thousands)	Change in the period (thousands)	**Percentage growth (or decline) per annum) (percent)**
	EMPLOYMENT CATEGORY				
1.1	Corporate Managers and Senior Officials	65	67	2	**0.2**
1.2	Production Managers	495	472	-23	**-0.4**
1.3	Functional Managers	999	1287	288	**2.3**
1.4	Quality and Customer Care Managers	54	67	13	**1.9**
1.5	Financial Institution and Office Managers	345	325	-19	**-0.5**
1.6	Managers in Distribution, Storage and Retailing	540	471	-69	**-1.2**
1.7	Protective Service Officers	41	37	-5	**-1.1**
1.8	Health and Social Services Managers	129	165	36	**2.2**
1	**Corporate Managers, Total**	**2669**	**2891**	**222**	**0.7**
2.1	Managers in Farming, Horticulture, Forestry and Fishing	35	23	-12	**-3.8**
2.2	Managers and Proprietors in Hospitality and Leisure Services	365	306	-58	**-1.6**
2.3	Managers and Proprietors in other Service Industries	578	498	-80	**-1.3**
2	**Managers / Proprietors in Agriculture and Services**	**978**	**827**	**-151**	**-1.5**
3.1	Science Professionals	86	91	5	**0.5**
3.2	Engineering Professionals	472	587	115	**2**
3.3	Information and Communication Technology Professionals	337	469	132	**3**
3	**Science and Technology Professionals, Total**	**985**	**1147**	**252**	**2.3**
4	**Health Professionals, Total**	**244**	**339**	**95**	**3**
5.1	Teaching and Research Professionals	1137	1385	248	**1.8**
5.2	Research Professionals	70	79	9	**1.1**
5	**Teaching and Research Professionals, Total**	**1206**	**1463**	**257**	**1.8**
6.1	Legal Professionals	126	206	80	**4.6**
6.2	Business and Statistical Professionals	271	425	154	**4.2**
6.3	Architects, Town Planners, Surveyors	133	139	6	**0.4**
6.4	Public Service Professionals	142	171	28	**1.7**
6.5	Librarians and Related Professionals	37	30	-8	**-2**
6	**Business and Public Service professionals, Total**	**710**	**971**	**261**	**2.9**
7.1	Science and Engineering Technicians	204	200	-4	**-0.2**
7.2	Draughtspersons and Building Inspectors	120	88	-31	**-2.7**
7.3	IT Service Delivery Occupations	77	114	37	**3.6**
7	**Science and Technology Associate Professionals, Total**	**401**	**402**	**1**	**0**

	Detailed employment growth projections				
	Table 2				
		1999	2010		
8.1	Health Associate Professionals	656	786	130	**1.7**
8.2	Therapists	58	69	12	**1.7**
8.3	Social Welfare Associate Professionals	170	249	79	**3.6**
8	**Health and Social Welfare Professionals, Total**	**884**	**1105**	**221**	**2.1**
9	**Protective Service Occupations**	**268**	**322**	**54**	**1.7**
10.1	Artistic and Literary Occupations	182	234	52	**2.3**
10.2	Design Associate Professionals	104	137	33	**2.5**
10.3	Media Associate Professionals	175	230	55	**2.5**
10.4	Sports and Fitness Occupations	37	45	9	**2**
10	**Culture, Media and Sports Occupations, Total**	**498**	**646**	**149**	**2.4**
11.1	Transport Associate Professionals	55	50	-5	**-0.9**
11.2	Legal Associate Professionals	36	49	12	**2.7**
11.3	Business and Finance Associate Professionals	354	466	112	**2.5**
11.4	Sales and Related Associate Professionals	534	634	100	**1.6**
11.5	Conservation Associate Professionals	10	11	1	**0.9**
11.6	Public Service and Other Associate Professionals	404	547	142	**2.8**
11	**Business and Public Service Associate Professionals, Total**	**1393**	**1756**	**363**	**2.1**
12.1	Administrative / Clerical Occupations: Government and Related Organisations	582	538	-44	**-0.7**
12.2	Administrative / Clerical Occupations: Finance	1060	1204	144	**1.2**
12.3	Administrative / Clerical Occupations: Records	646	687	41	**0.6**
12.4	Administrative / Clerical Occupations: Communications	111	115	4	**0.3**
12.5	Administrative / Clerical Occupations: General	505	520	15	**0.3**
12	**Administrative / Clerical Occupations, Total.**	**2905**	**3065**	**160**	**0.5**
13	**Secretarial and Related Occupations, Total**	**1141**	**1038**	**-104**	**-0.9**
14	**Agricultural Trades, Total**	**328**	**290**	**-39**	**-1.1**
15.1	Metal Forming, Welding and Related Trades	211	174	-37	**-1.7**
15.2	Metal Machining, Fitting and Instrument Making Trades	459	392	-67	**-1.4**
15.3	Vehicle Trades	298	283	-15	**-0.5**
15.4	Electrical Trades	577	582	5	**0.1**

	Detailed employment growth projections				
	Table 2				
		1999	2010		
15	**Skilled Metal and Electrical Trades, Total**	**1545**	**1432**	**-114**	**-0.7**
16.1	Construction and Building Trades	765	705	-61	**-0.7**
16.2	Building Trades	235	231	-4	**-0.2**
16	**Skilled Construction and Building Trades, Total**	**1001**	**936**	**-65**	**-0.6**
17.1	Textiles and Garments Trades	81	53	-29	**-3.9**
17.2	Printing Trades	121	119	-2	**-0.2**
17.3	Food Preparation Trades	525	552	28	**0.5**
17.4	Skilled Trades N.E.C.	178	202	24	**1.2**
17	**Textiles, Printing and Other Skilled Trades, Total**	**905**	**926**	**21**	**0.2**
18.1	Healthcare and Related Personal Services	709	1059	349	**3.7**
18.2	Childcare and Related Personal Services	306	431	125	**3.2**
18.3	Animal Care Services	19	16	-4	**-1.9**
18	**Caring Personal Service Occupations, Total**	**1034**	**1505**	**471**	**3.5**
19.1	Leisure and Travel Service Occupations	195	331	135	**4.9**
19.2	Hairdressers and Related Occupations	224	322	98	**3.3**
19.3	Housekeeping Occupations	125	62	-63	**-6.2**
19.4	Personal Services Occupations N.E.C.	15	20	5	**2.4**
19	**Leisure and Other Personal Service Occupations, Total**	**560**	**735**	**174**	**2.5**
20.1	Sales Assistants and Retail Cashiers	1463	1675	211	**1.2**
20.2	Sales Related Occupations	250	211	-39	**-1.5**
20	**Sales Occupations, Total**	**1714**	**1886**	**172**	**0.9**
21	**Customer Service Occupations, Total**	**101**	**107**	**6**	**0.5**
22.1	Process Operatives	467	475	7	**0.1**
22.2	Plant and Machine Operatives	333	262	-71	**-2.1**
22.3	Assemblers and Routine Operatives	558	501	-57	**-1**
22.4	Construction Operatives	141	135	-5	**-0.4**
22	**Process, Plant and Machine Operatives, Total**	**1499**	**1373**	**-126**	**-0.8**
23.1	Transport Drivers and Operatives	804	863	59	**0.6**
23.2	Mobile Machine Drivers and Operatives	143	106	-36	**-2.6**
23	**Transport and Mobile Machine Drivers and Operatives, Total**	**947**	**969**	**23**	**0.2**

	Detailed employment growth projections				
	Table 2				
		1999	2010		
24.1	Elementary Occupations: Agricultural Trades Related	106	74	-32	**-3.2**
24.2	Elementary Occupations: Construction and Related Trades	173	157	-16	**-0.9**
24.3	Elementary Occupations: Process and Plant Related	342	299	-43	**-1.2**
24.4	Elementary Occupations: Goods Handling and Storage Related	409	478	68	**1.4**
24	**Elementary Occupations: Trades, Plant and Storage Related, Total**	**1030**	**1007**	**-23**	**-0.2**
25.1	Elementary Occupations: Clerical Related	412	408	-3	**-0.1**
25.2	Elementary Occupations: Personal Services Related	845	742	-103	**-1.2**
25.3	Elementary Occupations: Cleansing Services	880	670	-211	**-2.5**
25.4	Elementary Occupations: Security and Safety Services	457	618	161	**2.8**
25.5	Elementary Occupations: Sales Related	95	97	1	**0.1**
25	**Elementary Occupations: Clerical and Services Related, Total**	**2690**	**2535**	**-154**	**-0.5**
	All occupations	27546	29673	2127	**0.7**
	Source: Warwick Institute for Employment Research, Projections of Occupations and Qualifications, 2000/2001, Tables 4.6				

Chapter eleven summary

☑ **The growth or decline of the job you chose will have a major effect on your career. Aim for growth if at all possible.**

☑ **Read weekly or monthly publications to get an up to date view on the prospects for the job that interests you.**

Next ➔➔

In the last part of this first section of the book, we investigate what sort of future you would like to have and how different jobs can give you different amounts of opportunity.

12

Future Career Opportunities, Money and Lifestyle

Some jobs can lead to a huge number of opportunities for your future career, while others take you down a narrow path quite early on. The trend in the employment market now is for people to change jobs and even entire careers much more than they used to. People want freedom and choice. There are career paths that give you this freedom and choice and others that do not. If you are at all unsure about the career choice that you are making then try very hard to keep to jobs that allow you to change your direction easily.

Think about transferable skills. If you are doing a job where the skills could be used in very many other jobs then you will have more freedom in your career. But if you are in a job that is very specialised and your skills are only relevant to that job, then it will be much harder for you to make a change.

Here are a couple of examples.

1 – A job in accountancy

Becoming a qualified accountant trains you to be able to analyse the accounts and finance of any company in the country, and with a little more training and international experience, almost any company in the world. It also positions you well to understand the business of any of these firms. That means that you have incredibly easily transferable skills. You can work for almost any firm on the planet with your skills.

You can move between industry sectors, you can move out of

direct accounting or finance work and into the actual management and business of a firm. You can choose big paying city firms or easier lifestyle rural firms. Put quite simply, you have a lot of choice. And because there is a lot of choice, people are always moving jobs, which creates more opportunity, which makes moving jobs easier and faster.

2 – A job in research into a specialised branch of nuclear physics
Whether in industry or in academia, the skills learned are going to be quite narrow. Most of the businesses in the world don't involve nuclear physics. A young nuclear physicist with good communication and personal skills could branch out into a different career line but he or she would be very likely to start at the bottom of the pile. The core skills learned are not very transferable. An older highly specialised nuclear physicist could quite simply be stuck in his or her line of work.

The more your job involves general and transferable skills, the wider your choice will be in the future. Keeping your opportunities open will allow you to have much more choice over the money and lifestyle that you want in the future as well as choice of the work you are doing. Look at the skills that you will learn in the job(s) you are considering and think about how transferable they may be. That can be a hard question if you don't have much work experience. Try to talk to people who have some years of experience and see what they think. Ask them if they think your proposed job would give you wide future opportunities or not.

The usual reason why people want to have a wide choice of future opportunities is to be able to have some control over what they want in the future in terms of money and lifestyle. Let's have a closer look at money and lifestyle.

Money

Money isn't everything, but it is the main reason why we go to work. As mentioned previously, we don't go there to look at the wallpaper.

It is tempting to go for the job that offers the biggest salary, and there's nothing wrong with that, if the job fits. But even then you should look at earning potential and not just the starting salary.

Earning potential

Some jobs pay a good starting salary but don't give very good pay rises over the years, whereas others have moderate starting salaries but can pay really well later.

Whether a starting salary is sixteen or seventeen thousand a year doesn't make that much difference to your spending power or lifestyle. The extra thousand is more of a confidence boost than anything else. But when you're thirty-five years old, you might be earning thirty thousand instead of sixty for the same amount of effort.

Find out how much the older people earn in the line of work you are looking at. It can be difficult to find out about earning potential, and of course it depends very largely on how well you do in your career. There is a good deal of salary information on the web and it is best to start there because books with salary information go out of date quite quickly. Have a look at **www.prospects.ac.uk**.

The best thing you can do is to talk to as many people as you can in different jobs. Don't ask them directly how much they earn – be as tactful as you can. If you drive to visit a company, check out what sort of cars are in the car park – it's a good indication of your earning potential with that company.

Lifestyle

Predicting the lifestyle you want can be hard. But when you choose a job you are making a decision that has a massive effect on your future lifestyle. Take some time to think about it.

Here's a list of words, circle the ones that are most important to you. Don't circle all of them – unfortunately it doesn't work like that!

BMWs and Mercedes	Love
Big houses with jacuzzi's and maids	A house that's big enough
A chalet in St Tropez	Children

Divorce lawyers	Free time
Early retirement	Friends
Expensive holidays	Being at home
Being at work	Hobbies
Expensive clothes	Families
Nannies	Relaxation
Stress	Being at your (future) daughter's birthday party rather than being at work

There's no hidden message in the list, it's just a few words to start you thinking about the reality of different business lifestyles. For most people, big money comes at a cost. It costs your free time and your energy. It costs quite a few marriages. The people who are truly happy earning huge salaries are the ones who just love being at work. The big salary is a by-product; they do the job because they love it.

How much money do you need and are you prepared to do what it takes to get it? We can't pretend to be able to answer this question for you. Only you can. Write down what you think you want in ten and twenty years. Try to be realistic. Think of some friends, relatives or colleagues who are older than you who have a life that you admire.

In ten years, I would like:

In twenty years, I would like:

If you are not very sure, then try to leave yourself choice. If you choose a job that gives you a wide range of career options later on you can probably change your job and alter your lifestyle according to what you want. But if you take a very narrow career line, it can be hard to change, you can be stuck in that line and that lifestyle. Fine if it's what you want, but frustrating if it's not. Always research the future career opportunities that are available from any particular job that you are looking at.

One last point about money. If you want to be seriously rich, then you need to have your own business. You need equity. People don't get seriously rich earning salaries, they can become well off and comfortable, but not independently rich.

The people who have made the huge killings are people who gained some experience working for other companies, left, and started or bought a business themselves and then grew it into a success story. It's not an easy path, and some try it and lose everything they have, but bear it in mind. If your aspirations are towards making a really massive amount of money you need to think about other people working for you, not you working for them.

Chapter twelve summary

☑ **Some jobs allow you to choose your future from a wide range of possibilities. If the skills that you learn are transferable then moving job can be relatively easy and changing your whole career is possible.**

☑ **You can redefine your money and lifestyle goals at almost any point and change your work to achieve them.**

☑ **If your job teaches you narrow skills then only a narrow range of jobs will be open to you. You will probably have to retrain and/or start again at the bottom of the pile to change your career. This can seriously constrain your options in terms of money and lifestyle.**

☑ **If you are not very clear about what you will want in the future try to keep your options as open as you can.**

☑ **Very few people manage to earn a really big salary and have a relaxed lifestyle. It's usually one or the other. Think about which you want, and of course, you can achieve a compromise between the two.**

13

Part 1 Conclusion

Now that you have read through this section, it's up to you to go out and look at the jobs that interest you. Look in your careers library, look on the net and talk to as many people as you can. Don't drift into a career 'because it sounds nice'. Choose it because it's right for you.

You know what your Job Activities are, and that is a huge step towards making the right job choice, and now you know all the other important factors that you need to think about in choosing a career.

Look at each job that you are considering in turn and try to be objective about it in all the areas we have gone through.

- Find out what the real activities are in the jobs you are looking at, don't be misled by glamorised images or reputations. Make sure the activities are at least a reasonable match to your JAs. If they are not you could well be unhappy in that job.

- Think about how the job – and its activities – fit with your original dreams or ambitions.

- Be realistic about the influence of your parents' occupation and opinions.

- Judge whether you have the right qualifications for the job.

- Relate your previous work experience to the new job and see how much of your experience is relevant, how many of your skills are transferable, and whether the JAs of the old job were right for you.

- Make sure you know the demographic structure of the new firm or industry. Make sure you fit amongst the people with whom you are going to work;

- Definitely check out how trends in the employment market will affect your prospects in this job. Think very seriously before entering a shrinking market.

- Find out what the future opportunities of the job are. Will you learn transferable skills or narrow skills? Be realistic about the money and lifestyle that you want. Get to know the job well enough to see if it will provide what you want now and in the future. If you are not sure exactly what you will want in the future go for something that gives you choice later on.

Put some effort into finding out about the jobs. You are going to be there for a long time. Reading a couple of glossy brochures will not provide enough information to answer the questions that you have. By far the best thing you can do is to talk to someone who is in the industry you are looking at. You can ask them all the questions we have gone through and they will be able to give you direct answers to most of them.

Good luck with your career choice. It is not an easy decision but you are armed with everything you need to make the right choice for you now.

Well, that's the end of Part One. When you have chosen the job(s) that you are going for you have to go out and get the offers. That's what Part Two of the book is all about.

Part Two

How to Land the Job Offer - CVs, Applications and Interviews

Part 2 Introduction

Now that you have chosen your career direction it's time to go out and get the job. CVs, interviews and applications can seem like a bit of a 'black art'. It's easy to feel that everyone else knows more about it all than you do. We break this black art down into simple easy to manage parts. Then we put all the parts together in the right order and we end up with a well organised, easy to follow method to deal with finding vacancies, writing CVs and applications and performing well in interviews. You can work through it on your own, or, together with a friend or adviser.

Here's a diagram to show you how it all fits together.

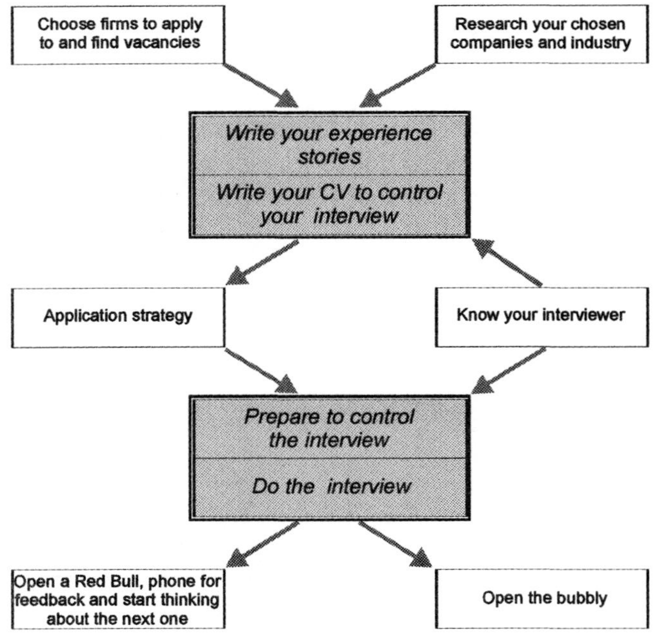

Remember the Five Ps

No one is good enough to bang out a quick CV, throw a suit on and turn up at an interview. The most successful applicants are the ones who do the best preparation. The jobs do not necessarily go to the candidate with the most natural talent. They go to the candidate who presents him or herself best to the interviewer, and that comes down to preparation.

Always remember the five Ps when dealing with CVs and interviews.

Prior Preparation Prevents Poor Performance

14

How to Find Vacancies and Which Companies to Apply to

Once you have chosen the type of job you want, you need to find companies that are actually looking for new people. This can be as easy as buying a newspaper and opening the job section or as difficult as finding a needle in a haystack.

Here are the more obvious places to look:

- school or university career library
- newspaper job sections
- web pages of relevant companies.

Here are other sources that can be very helpful.

- University 'Milk Rounds' – this is when companies make presentations to university members and set up interviews for likely candidates.
- Develop your own network of contacts.
- Look at recruitment consultancies (usually only interested in outstanding graduates or professionals with more than three years experience).
- Visit job search websites – there are many on the net. You can simply enter 'jobs' in a search engine and go from there. Popular sites are **www.monster.co.uk, www.reed.co.uk, www.cityjobs.co.uk, www.jobsite.co.uk, www.jobs.fish4.co.uk, www.topdogjobs.co.uk, www.topjobs.co.uk**

- Attend career fairs – enquire about upcoming events at school or university careers library or your local job centre.
- Read trade magazines.

When you find a firm that you like the sound of, don't apply to them immediately. You need to do careful research and you need to tailor your CV to their requirements.

Networking for job contacts

Networking is really a fancy name for making friends and contacts in a business context. Creating a good network is absolutely crucial to any successful professional and can be just as important for finding your job in the first place.

The term networking is a bit clichéd and the concept can seem awkward at first. If you do your networking professionally, then people will be very happy to talk to you.

It is really no problem to ask for help – in fact one of the first qualities that employers are looking for in new recruits is that they can identify when they need help and ask for it. Just remember to be honest and listen openly to advice. Always be prepared to offer any favour in return to a network contact or friend who helps you. That's what it's all about.

When I left college, a friend and I were both trying to get jobs abroad. It's difficult for a fresh graduate with no real experience. Companies don't want to pay all the costs to move someone without a good track record. I was writing letters and sending CVs by the kilo to no avail. My buddy didn't approach it like that. He spent ages on the phone talking to everyone that he could think of. People in the hall of residence were getting fed up with him because he wouldn't get off the pay phone. Eventually he got in touch with a friend of a relative who worked for a US firm. He phoned them up and it turned out that they could not get enough graduate recruits in his particular subject that year. They asked him for a CV. He sent it and then phoned them to follow up. The guy on the other end said, *'We'll pay ya 38 grand a year, ya want the job or not?'*

That was his interview. Simple as that. One syllable required. Yes!

Don't expect it to be that easy – I have never heard of anything quite so simple before or since then, but it did happen to him. He was lucky, but he was lucky because he kept pushing, kept phoning, kept asking. He kept networking.

The world does not arrive conveniently at the front door. We have to go out and push for things to happen. Usually it doesn't fall into place on the first attempt. Don't stop trying until you get an offer, no matter how long it takes.

Hearing the word 'No' is not a reason to give up. It's a reason to move forwards.

When you have identified people with whom you would like to network, you can either write to them, telephone them or organise a meeting via an intermediary.

Here are some people you could try:

- friends of your parents
- family relatives and their friends
- local town acquaintances, Doctor, Bank Manager, etc
- parents of your friends
- co-workers and managers of any previous jobs.

You can offer to buy them a coffee or a beer one evening and ask as much as you can about the industry itself and of course whether they know of any vacancies. If they don't know they might know someone who does, and are usually happy to ask on your behalf.

You may find it a bit embarrassing at first to set up these meetings, but your network contact will almost certainly be glad to help. Each one of them had to find their first job once and they will remember what it was like. Many people are quite flattered to be asked – it implies that they are important and connected, and professional people like that.

Finding vacancies – summary

There are many different sources of job advertisements. Look at as many of them as you can. If you only look in one area, you might miss some good opportunities.

Try to create your own network of contacts. It can be hard work but if you make the right contact, your job search can be over very quickly.

Which companies to apply to

Larger companies are more likely to take on fresh recruits from school or university than small ones. If you don't have much or any previous experience, it may be better to aim for larger firms that run specialised recruitment and training programmes. Smaller firms prefer to take people with at least a couple of years experience as they often don't have the resources to train people in the very early stages of professional life. It is also very useful if your first company is large enough to have a recognisable name and a good reputation. Nowadays very few people stay with their first firm for life. When you want to move, it is much easier if potential employers are familiar with the firm you were working for.

Look through the following list of questions when you are considering applying to a firm:

- Is it large?
- Is it growing?
- Is it profitable?
- Does it have good training schemes?
- Is it international?
- Does it pay well (now and later)?

Find out if the company is growing or not. Growing companies take on more recruits and have more room for early promotions. There are several things you can do to find out if a firm is growing.

- Ask them in your interview.
- Look at the last four or five years published accounts, did turnover grow or not, did the head count grow? (Many firms have their accounts on the net.)
- Look at the industry as a whole – is it growing or not? You can

find this out by reading *The Economist* regularly, the business sections of newspapers, asking friends and network contacts. Check chapter 11 in Part One of this book.

If you want an international career, it is much easier to join a large international company and to move abroad internally than to find a job on your own abroad. You can find out about international opportunities in the interview stages. Many larger companies run specialised international placement schemes to move employees between their offices around the world.

Within your chosen field of work there will be firms with more prestigious names and some with a lesser reputation. For your first position it's best to aim for the most prestigious name. A good name makes it easier to move to another firm later on. A prestigious name should be a significant factor in your company ranking. People talk of 'blue chip' companies. Try to aim for a 'blue chip' firm

The best thing you can do if you are wondering whether to apply to a firm is to talk to a recent recruit, someone who has been there a year or two. Go through your school or university alumni contacts and see if there is someone you could call. They can tell you what it's really like in just a quick phone call.

Chapter fourteen – summary

☑ **Make a judgement of each company that you consider. How attractive are they? Firms in the same industry can be quite different to work for depending on their size, growth, success etc. You need to be able to rank them for your application strategy.**

Next ➔➔

Now we will look at how actually to apply.

15

Application Strategy

Once you have identified companies that look good, you need to decide how many to approach and when to approach them.

Some people send out standard letters by the hundred hoping that if they splatter the whole planet with their CV, someone will read it, and some people send just a couple or even only one application to the company they have set their hearts on.

If you set your heart on a firm too early, they'll probably break it for you. Firms can be like that. And if you take the splatter gun approach, the firms will probably splatter you right back because you can't put any company-specific focus into a hundred CVs at a time.

An average job seeker may have to send out more than fifty applications and go through quite a few interviews to receive one good offer. It's a tough game so be prepared to receive some 'Dear Johns' (letters that start, 'Dear John, Unfortunately …' etc).

Applicants who never get rejected are usually underselling themselves. They could have found a much better job if they had been prepared to take a few knocks on the way.

So, make a list of as many firms as you can that are attractive to you. (Thirty is a good number. Ten is not enough). Rank them most attractive first and so on. Apply to around eight initially. But not just the first eight. Apply to numbers one to four and nine to twelve. This might sound a bit odd, but there's a good reason.

You learn a lot in going through your first round of applications. If a firm rejects you, there is a long wait before you can re-apply with any hope of success (minimum six months). You may well be a better prepared candidate when you make your second round of applications – so don't risk blowing your top eight in the first shot. Let firms nine to twelve teach you things you need to know to land an offer from number six.

Always ask for the maximum possible feedback when you have applied to a firm and been rejected. Often they can tell you one or two specific points that are absolutely crucial. Your CV might not include the right qualifications, or if you get to interview, there might be a problem with your technique that you can easily sort out.

A rejection is a perfect learning opportunity. Don't waste it feeling sorry for yourself and blunder on making the same mistakes. Take a deep breath and phone for feedback and change your approach for the next round. Interview and CV coaches are expensive. Application feedback is free, and HR departments are happy to provide it.

If companies five to eight and thirteen to sixteen don't get you anywhere then it's onto the next round. Keep going. Rejections don't mean that you are a bad candidate. They mean you have to keep looking and keep learning. Getting the right job for you is about the fit between you and the job. Just because the recruitment staff thought you didn't fit one particular job doesn't mean you will not fit the next one.

I applied to McKinsey's once. (They are the big hitter in the management consultancy world). They wrote back saying, thanks, but no thanks. I didn't even read the whole letter. I found it a while later, and they recommended that I do an MBA. So I did. I still didn't get into McKinsey's, but I did work for one of their competitors. It was good advice.

Chapter fifteen summary

☑ **Select a reasonably large number of firms and apply to them with a strategy.**

☑ **You learn a lot by going through the first set of applications.**

☑ **Always ask for feedback if you were not accepted, this information could be the key to landing the next offer.**

16

Research

It's extremely important that you research the industry, company and job that you're aiming for before you start making applications. People who arrive at the interview and have not done their research will not impress the interviewer.

The interviewers will always ask questions to test your research. They want to hire people who know what they are getting into, people who have a good chance of enjoying the job, working well and staying for at least a few years. You can stand out very clearly above the other applicants by going further with your research.

Let's have a look first at what information you need to find, and then where you can get it.

What you need to find out

You probably know the basics of your target industry already, but if not, the following bullets show you what to look for.

For a primary industry (extraction of raw materials, e.g. offshore oil drilling and production, or coal mining):

- What is the product, different types and grades of product?
- What technology and equipment are used?
- Find out about storage and transportation.
- Who are the clients, and what do they produce with this raw material?
- Look into structure and state of the market for the product (e.g. the crude oil market).

- How large is the industry?
- Who are the main competitors?

For a secondary industry (making products from materials e.g. the car industry or computer manufacture) look into the following.

- What materials are used?
- What processes and technology are used?
- What are the products?
- Who are the clients, how do they benefit from the product?
- What distribution network is there?
- What is the the market place (e.g. the market for new cars)?
- How do they do their advertising?
- Who are the main competitors and what do their products offer?
- Look into the industry scale.

For a tertiary industry (service industries such as teaching, banking and accounting), check the following.

- What service do they offer?
- What knowledge do they need to offer the service?
- Who are the customers?
- Who are the main competitors?
- How do they market their services?
- What is the scale of the industry?

Here are some other interesting areas to look into if you want to really impress your interviewer.

- What is the company culture? (Refer to Chapter 23 in Part Three for information on culture.)
- Is there a company mission statement or vision?
- Who owns the company? (shareholder or partnership structure etc)
- Whether the company is successful or not, try to find out last year's profit.

- What really makes the money and what is support? (for example Dixons the electrical goods store makes very little profit from selling electrical goods – the money comes from selling warranty policies).

Don't limit your research to ideas on this list – almost anything you can find out could be useful. Better research shows that you can work hard and are interested in learning. And when you get to the interview, show them what you know. Put your research right there on the table.

Where you can find it

There are many places to search for all this information. Again let's start with the more obvious sources.

- Read the annual report, (you can download it from the net or write to the company secretary and ask him or her to send you one. Get the address from the net).
- Check the company recruitment brochure.
- Check the company product brochure.
- Read the company website – make sure you know it very well.
- If the company has retail shops or products, visit them, pay close attention and buy and use the products if they are not too expensive. If the products are expensive, try to read consumer tests on the products, for example in 'Which?' magazine.

Here are some further sources of information:

- Check the business section of newspapers and magazines.
- Check the competitors' web pages.
- Call a stock broker and ask for an information package so that you can see if you want to buy shares (if it is a public company).
- Anyone you know who works for the company or one of the direct competitors can be an invaluable source. Go through

school and college alumni lists to see if there is anyone who works there or has worked there in the past that you could contact.

Start a file for each company you are researching and keep everything in it.

Case study on research

David Shorling is in his third year at university studying Chemistry. He wants to get a job in accountancy with a firm that will sponsor him through his professional accountancy exams and hopefully provide a promising future. He has heard of a big firm called Price Waterhouse Coopers, or PWC.

He knows he has to do a lot of research before he applies to them. Here are a couple of his private thoughts...

'Where do I even start? There is so much stuff to find out, I'll never remember it all! I bet if I spend days on end learning it they'll just ask about something else.'

OK David. Start with a cup of tea. That's always a good idea. Maybe a pack of Hobnobs too. Then have a look at pages 91/92 where we have a list of things to find out. Do it bit by bit. And they will ask about it in the interview. They always do.

Accounting is a tertiary industry, they don't produce anything physical, they provide a service – so take the list of info for a tertiary industry and the general list from pages 92/93.

The list for a tertiary industry looks like this.

- What service do they offer?
- What knowledge do they need to offer the service?
- Who are the customers?
- Who are the main competitors?
- How do they market their services?
- What is the scale of the business?

And here's the list of further information that we had earlier.

- What is the company and culture?
- Is there a company mission statement or vision?

- Who owns the company? (shareholder or partnership structure)
- Whether the company is successful or not, try to find out last year's profit.
- What really makes the money and what is support?

On with David's story:

'So now I've got a list, and a cup of tea. Great, what's next?' thinks David.

The Hobnobs. And then the Internet.

Some firms have great websites that will tell you almost everything you need, and others don't have much. If they don't have a website at all then you probably don't want a job there anyway.

David found a ton of information on their website. The services are almost endless, but audit, general accounting advice and tax advice are very prominent.

The knowledge they use comes from two main sources. The accounting legislation, (the law) and their own knowledge. Buzzwords like **balance sheets, profit and loss, tax, income, expenditure** and **financial risk** come up all the time. The pages on recruitment and training talked about the accounting exams as well.

Their potential customers are almost every limited company in the UK, for the UK offices and likewise for their other offices all over the world.

They didn't talk much about their main competitors on the web site.

They market their services through their reputation, through advertising, through business lectures and presentations etc.

The scale is very large. They have thousands of employees in the UK.

There was a lot more info on the site that David printed out and put in his file. But he didn't really find out much info for the list of further information.

'Culture – what the hell is that anyway?' he says to himself. It's a good question and there is no easy answer. To get a good idea of the culture of a firm or industry, you probably have to meet someone who has worked in it and ask them.

'My Granddad used to go on about accountants – maybe I'll ask him,' thinks David.

Good idea. Obviously it might not be the most up to date info, but accounting culture probably hasn't changed that much in the last couple of decades either.

Granddad came up with the goods. He has a friend, Bob, who is a retired accountant and he asked David and Bob to come round one afternoon for a chat. Bob described what it's like in an accounting firm, and how partnerships are different from shareholder-owned companies. He was really useful, more than David had expected. He could answer all the points that David couldn't find on the internet. Granddad also gave David twenty quid to take his girlfriend out on Saturday as well. *'Not a bad afternoon.'* thought David on his way home.

Chapter sixteen summary

☑ **Research into your chosen companies and industry is crucial.**

☑ **You will probably not receive any offers if you have not done your research.**

☑ **You can separate yourself from other applicants by going further with your research.**

Next ➔➔

Now that we've had a look at research we're going to move onto how to prepare your CV and application to send to the firms, and then we'll work on interview technique. But, before we do that let's have a think about the interviewers themselves.

17

Know Your Interviewers

In an interview, you are essentially trying to sell your talent, energy and time to your target company. You are trying to sell all of this for a considerable period of time. You are trying to persuade them to buy you instead of the other applicants.

Whenever you are trying to sell, you need to know who the buyers are. You need to think about what they want. The buyers in this situation are your interviewers and possibly other members of the recruitment team in the company. So let's look at typical interviewers and think about what they are looking for.

The interview process usually consists of at least two rounds with possibly more than one interview in each round.

Often the first interview is conducted in the Human Resources (HR) department of the company, in which case you will probably be dealing with an experienced interviewer. The second and further interviews are usually conducted in the relevant department or team of the company that you wish to join. Your interviewer may be the department manager or his or her deputy.

Interview topics usually relate to one or more of the following three areas:

- **ability** – can you do the job?
- **motivation** – do you want to do the job?
- **cultural fit** – will you fit into this company and department?

Some interviewers know about these three areas and you will be able to see how they probe each one. Others are not aware of the three areas explicitly but the underlying concepts are still present. Employers find it reasonably easy to predict ability and motivation – your school and university grades are quite a good indication – but they find it very hard to predict cultural fit. Emphasise how you would fit in with them as much as you can.

Here is a more detailed look at each interviewer.

Interviewer 1 from the Human Resources (HR) department

An HR department interviewer may have had some interview training and will probably have enough time to prepare well for your interview. Recruitment and interviewing are probably a core part of his or her job.

This means that he or she will have thoroughly read your application and may ask quite detailed questions about your letter, CV and your aspirations.

The HR interviewer is probably not an expert in your specific field and so will not ask particularly detailed technical questions. He or she will usually concentrate more on the areas of motivation and fit, and will be interested in the following:

- personal presentation and manner (fit)
- maturity (fit)
- evidence that you can work hard (ability and motivation)
- communication skills (ability and fit)
- evidence that you can work well in teams (fit)
- is this the right level of job for you? Are you likely to be satisfied and stay with the firm? (fit and motivation)
- evidence that you can fit into their particular company's culture (fit)
- are you helpful, happy and positive or negative or aggressive? (fit)
- do they like you? (fit) (a common question an interviewer will ask him or herself is, would I like to sit in an economy class aeroplane seat next to this person for 15 hours).

This interview will probably be well structured and the questions will flow smoothly.

Some firms hire external interviewers for the first round of interviews. Their interview style is usually similar to the HR interviewer. In fact you might not even be told that the interviewer does not work fulltime for the firm.

Interviewer 2, from the department or team

This person is busy. He or she may have already been to three meetings that morning and has a busy afternoon followed by dinner with a new client. He or she may have read your CV on the train that morning or in a quick coffee break, and probably did not read your application form or cover letter.

Some interviewers from the departments are experienced and skilled in interviewing and some are not. If this interviewer seems nervous, he or she probably is. This may be a first interview sitting on the other side of the table and he or she may be completely unprepared. Don't worry, you are prepared and can present yourself well, even to a relatively poor interviewer.

The interview may not be very well structured, in other words the questions may seem unrelated to each other and some may seem irrelevant. If you have prepared your experience stories well (see next section) and you have **primed your CV** with the right invitations to bring out your stories this is your chance to control the interview. You make the interviewer's job much easier if interesting questions leap out of the CV on a quick read through.

The department interviewer is probably less likely to separate questions directly into ability, motivation and fit, but the three topics are still there beneath the surface. The department interviewer usually concentrates more on ability than the HR interviewer, but he or she is still interested in motivation and fit.

The topics will usually include the following:

- Does the applicant (you) have the skills and/or qualifications to do the job? (ability)
- Can you use the qualifications? (i.e. did you pass your exams by last minute cramming and then forget the lot, or do you really know and understand what you have learned?) (ability)

- Do you have relevant work experience, and did you do well in it? (ability)
- Are you a problem solver? (ability and motivation)
- Will you fit into the culture of this department? (fit)
- Do I like you? (fit)

Chapter seventeen summary

☑ **You need to know the people you are dealing with to be able to impress them.**

☑ **When you have a good idea of what the interviewers are looking for you can prepare your material in a much more attractive manner.**

☑ **Always keep in mind what the interviewers are looking for.**

Next ➔➔

Now we've looked at the people who will be reading your CV and conducting your interviews, we can move on to how to present yourself as a really attractive candidate – a candidate that the firm will want to interview. The first part of this is how to organise your background, education and previous work experience. We are going to use the technique of Experience Stories.

18

Experience Stories and CVs

Experience stories are the core of a system to design your CV, application and interview answers. You can control the whole process with good experience stories.

As the name suggests, the system is based on stories of your past experience. The stories are written to bring out the highlights of your past that are relevant to the job you are going for. The whole process of writing your application, CV and performing well in the interviews is centred on these stories. You can even have them in mind when you are doing your research. Good invitations to the experience stories stand out in your CV and give you the chance to set the agenda for your interview and control it. This is a huge advantage over those who are not in control and don't know what to expect.

Some applicants are terrified of trick questions in interviews. In reality most interviews have very few, if any trick questions. You get the job based on what we call the 'meat and potatoes' questions; your experience, your qualifications, questions on your subject area and your personal presentation. Concentrate on your meat and potatoes, they get you the job. Then spend a bit of time learning how not to lose it on the rest.

Stories are a much more powerful way of relating information than descriptions. A story proves that you have done something. Look at the following example:

🕮 **Story** – when I was doing a summer job at Sainsbury's, I found it really interesting to see which workers got on well with the others and I tried hard to get on with everyone. I found it good fun even when we had to work very hard there.

◈ **Description** – I'm good with people, I'm perceptive and I work hard.

The story and the description essentially present the same points. The story shows that you have put the ideas into practice. It allows you to talk well of yourself indirectly, which means you come across as pleasant instead of arrogant or naïve. You infer gently that you are wonderful, but you don't say it directly. The description is blunt, and not based on anything that is tangible to the recruiter or interviewer. It could come across as arrogant. Anyone can sit there and say how wonderful they are. Here is another example:

🕮 **Story** – This book has helped many people to choose a career, get a job and lay the foundations for a really successful career. Quite a few readers also said it was fun to read.

◈ **Description** – I'm the best author in the world; eat your heart out, Stephen King.

That's extreme example, but I've heard comments in interviews that were just as bad. You can see clearly how the story is much nicer to read than the description.

The experience story method ensures that you can always perform well in your interviews even if you are nervous or worried. Your competitors who go in unprepared might just be lucky and pull off a good performance on the big day, but more likely they will under-perform. It is very difficult to bring all of your best points into an interview if you have not prepared for it.

Your application form or cover letter and your CV are 'primed' with invitations for the interviewer to ask questions that you can answer with these stories. Most interviewers are reasonably nice, and, as we have mentioned, often not particularly well prepared. As long as you have done your company and job research well enough, they will take up your invitations to lead into your stories.

In your research, try to look for between five and ten key areas or buzzwords that are central to the job that you are after. The keys can be training, qualifications, personal skills, technical know-how etc.

The interviewer is looking for matches between you and the requirements of the job. You write the experience stories specifically for each job you apply for. Take the aspects of your experience that are the closest match to the job buzzwords and build a story around it.

When the right time comes in the interview you can deliver these stories in a confident and polished manner that shows that you are an attractive candidate for this job, and you are the sort of person who pays attention, does your homework and can deliver the goods when called upon. You go in talking their language. And that is what employers want.

The first thing we will do is to look at a typical job and find around five to ten buzzwords or key areas. Buzzwords are not trivial – they express a shorthand or inside vocabulary of an industry. They are very powerful if used intelligently. Keep ability, motivation and *fit* in mind when choosing buzzwords. Try to touch on all three.

There are some buzzwords that will be relevant for almost every job. Remember the things that the HR interviewer was likely to want to see. The list was:

- communication skills
- personal presentation and manner
- maturity
- evidence that you can work hard
- evidence that you can fit into teams well
- is this the right level of job for you? Are you likely to be satisfied and stay with the firm?
- evidence that you can fit into their particular company's culture
- are you helpful, pleasant and positive or negative and aggressive?
- do they like you?

We can take a number of general buzzwords from this list, for example:

- **communication** (ability and fit)
- **work hard** (ability and motivation)
- **teams** (fit)
- fit into **culture** (fit)
- **positive** (fit and motivation).

When doing this for yourself, you take whichever buzzwords fit into a story about something that you have done.

Now let's look back to the case study where David was doing his research on an accountancy job. We will find another set of buzzwords for his job. The research showed that the following areas are very important to jobs in accountancy:

- balance sheet (ability)
- profit/loss (ability)
- income/expenditure (ability)
- financial risk (ability)
- tax (ability)
- exams (motivation and ability).

So, the complete list of buzzwords looks like this:

Balance sheet, profit/loss, income/expenditure, financial risk, tax, exams, communication, positive, work hard, teams, fit into culture.

If you are replying to an advertisement for a job there will be buzzwords in the advert. The recruiters will definitely be looking for these buzzwords in your CV. Try to include some of them if at all possible.

To write stories for David, we need to work as many of the words as possible into his stories of experience, background and education.

Writing experience stories and a CV is a little bit like the chicken and the egg. It's not obvious which one should come first. If you don't have a CV then start with the general CV suggested on page 117. Write some notes on a blank outline of this CV about your past. Then you can write the actual stories to fit to each section of your CV.

Whichever way you start, remember that you need to go through both your CV and your stories a few times to tie the two together properly.

Below is CV1 for David that was written before he had thought about experience stories and buzzwords. It is not a bad CV, it goes through his education and work history, but it does not make him look particularly interesting compared to any other applicant's CV, and it doesn't really make him look like a budding accountant. It includes ability but not much motivation or fit.

Compare it to CV2. You should be able to see a marked improvement. CV2 has been primed with buzzword invitations for an interviewer to ask about David's experience. He will now be able to respond to questions with stories, or answers, that demonstrate that his experience is relevant and attractive to a firm looking for trainee accountants. CV2 projects David as a candidate who is definitely interested in accounting and has made an effort to find out as much about it as he can.

CV 1

Curriculum Vitae

David Shorling

Job Objective Position as trainee accountant including training for full qualification.

Education and experience summary

Completing BSc in Chemistry, University of West Anglia, B,B,C at A level, summer work experience with Taylor and Long accountants in Guyton, Norfolk.

Work experience

Summer 2002 Worked for eight weeks with Taylor and Long accountants in Tax dept. Duties included checking Tax receipts and making coffee.

Summer 2001	Worked for eight weeks with Taylor and Long in the audit department. Duties included checking that forms were filled in completely and doing copying.
Summer 2000	Worked in Sainsbury's for six weeks stocking shelves.
Education	
University West Anglia	BSc in Chemistry, first year grade 2.2, second year grade 2.2, final year expected grade 2.1.
Norwich Secondary School	A levels Chemistry B, Physics B, Maths C GCSEs 1 A, 4 Bs, 3 Cs

Societies, sports and organisations attended

Captain of University second men's hockey team. Play for residence hall hockey and football team. Member of school debating society.

Languages, IT skills and other interests

Languages - Reasonable French, Basic German.
IT skills - comfortable using MS Office and Outlook.
Fly fishing (I make my own flies as well).

Contact Details

Address 8 The Rise, Little Burton, Norfolk, NRXXXX
Phone 0123 45678
Email David@UWAXXX.ac.uk

Now let's pep David's CV up a bit with buzzwords which will invite an interviewer to his experience stories.

CV 2

Curriculum Vitae

David Shorling

Job Objective Position as trainee accountant including training for full qualification.

Education and experience summary

Completing BSc in Chemistry, University of West Anglia, B,B,C at A level, summer work experience with Taylor and Long accountants in Guyton, Norfolk.

Work experience

Summer 2002 Worked for 8 weeks with Taylor and Long accountants in Tax dept. Worked with team of tax specialists to assess tax position of various clients. Enjoyed many tasks from detailed numerical work to simple things like making the coffee to help keep the team going when working late nights.

Summer 2001 Worked for 8 weeks with Taylor and Long in the Audit dept. I learned a great deal about balance sheets, asset valuations, profit and loss assessments, etc. I also learned about how necessary attention to detail is in audit work.

Summer 2000 Worked in Sainsbury's for 6 weeks. The work was not very intellectually demanding but looking back I can really appreciate the importance of stock control and the different cultures of the retail industry and the accounting industry.

Education

University West Anglia
BSc in Chemistry, first year grade 2.2, second year grade 2.2, final year expected grade 2.1.
Norwich Secondary School
A levels Chemistry B, Physics B, Maths C, GCSEs 1 A, 4 Bs, 3 Cs

Societies, sports and organisations attended
Captain of University second men's hockey team. I organise training and matches and am responsible for picking the team and making sure that we all get on well together. In spare time I play for residence hall hockey and football team. I was a keen member of the school debating society. This was a great opportunity to work on communication skills and public speaking.

Languages, IT skills and other interests
Languages - Reasonable French, Basic German.
IT skills - comfortable using MS Office and Outlook.
Fly fishing (I make my own flies as well).

Contact Details
Address 8 The Rise, Little Burton, Norfolk, NRXXXX
Phone 0123 45678
Email David@UWAXXX.ac.uk

Can you see the difference in the two CVs? The second one projects David as a motivated business person and accountant in the making. It is much easier for the interviewer to spot ability, motivation and fit. It gives the interviewer so many opportunities to ask directly about the qualities in a prospective employee that the firm will really want. David can respond with his stories, talking their language. The first CV merely lists what David has done. It does not put him forward as particularly interested in teams or balance sheets or any of the other buzzwords that we have found for an accounting interview.

A quick caution about loading your CV with buzzwords;

You must know enough about the topic to hold an intelligent conversation.

If you can't talk about the topic for at least 30 seconds, then don't put the word in your CV. People who try to bluff their way through detailed questions usually fail and don't get the job. You don't have to be an expert and you can study weak areas before the interview. Read textbooks, look around on the net or ask friends, but don't try to make it all up on the big day.

Now let's get into the real nitty gritty – the experience stories.

We will write a story for the main sections of David's CV to give you an example of how to do them. Often the interviewer will pick up on one of the buzzwords and ask you about it in more depth – so we prepare a sub-story to display your understanding of each of the buzzword topics.

It seems like a lot of work but it is important that you actually write your own stories word for word and rehearse them. You can ad lib as much as you want later, but you always need a safety net story that you can produce, no matter how nervous you are in an actual interview.

It takes time to do all of this preparation, but it really pays off. You have spent so many evenings doing homework or college work and the main objective was to land the right job. Every hour you put in now could allow you to highlight something that took you months or years to actually achieve. The interview for the job that you really want is the crucial time to show what you have done.

The most basic question in an interview is for the interviewer to look at your CV, find something that interests him or her and to ask, 'Could you tell me a bit about what you did at ...?'. There are many other types of questions, and we will deal with these later, in Chapter 20, but the 'could you tell me about ...?' question is the one we have in mind when writing the experience stories. You will always be able to use some of your stories in any style of interview, whether this exact question comes up or not.

An initial answer to a 'tell me about ...' question should be 15 to

30 seconds long. You want to develop a friendly interactive conversation, and not to give a 30 minute lecture.

We have prepared some example experience stories below from David's case study. These stories are combined with notes about writing the stories. Try to understand what is going on behind each story as you read it. Think about things that you have done, and imagine how you can make them sound interesting to an interviewer.

So, onto David's stories. Remember the buzzwords from the case study. We want to use the words reasonably often in his experience stories, but only where they fit naturally – we don't want to make it all sound too contrived.

The first section of David's CV talks about his eight weeks in the tax department of Taylor and Long. The CV has the following buzzwords in it:

- tax (*ability*)
- assess (*ability*)
- detailed numerical work (*ability and motivation*)
- help keep the team going (*motivation and fit*).

The interviewer is almost certain to ask about this work experience.

Interviewer

'So David, tell me a little about your time at Taylor and Long. You mentioned that you were in the Tax department – what were you doing there?'

For your first answer (and all others) you want to appear positive, buoyant, happy, motivated and so on. You want the interviewer to like you and to think that you are easy to get on with. First impressions count in interviews just as much as anywhere else. **Do not include anything negative or critical in the first story** (avoid it in the others as well). If the first part of your CV was not a positive experience for you then you need to either delete it, move it lower down or re-think the experience solely in terms of positive aspects. If you complain about something in the first moments, your interviewer will assume that you will continue complaining if they give you a job. They will not give you a job.

David

> *'Yes, I worked mostly on a project to help the Crow's Nest Crab Company to assess its tax position. I started by going through the invoices for the year and building a spreadsheet of all VAT paid. It was very detailed and it was nice to work alongside one of their recently recruited employees in the accounts department to find all the information. The project was on a tight deadline so we had to work quite a few late nights, but the team all got on together really well so it was actually good fun.'*

This initial answer has 93 words, that's about 30 seconds, which is a bit long, but okay. It still lets the interviewer become involved again before he or she can get bored.

The story includes buzzwords – *assess tax position, VAT, spreadsheets, work late nights* and *team got on together well* – five buzzwords which is quite a few, but it flows well. If you try to put more than five in a short story like this it may sound a bit contrived.

Usually the interviewer will want to investigate the story more deeply and will pick up one of the buzzwords. This first story has a mixture of technical buzzwords (ability) and soft skill (motivation and fit) buzzwords. This is a good idea as some interviewers may be more technically oriented, and some more interested in the soft skills. Having a bit of both in the story lets the interviewer pick up on either technical or non-technical – whichever he or she finds most interesting.

Let's go through a technical question first and a soft skills question second. It is all right to have a little longer answer for the sub-story if you have a good material to offer. The interviewer has asked for detail on a specific point. Between 20 and 30 seconds is appropriate (60 to 90 words).

Interviewer

> *'Umm, yes, that sounds great. Have you done a lot of spreadsheeting?'*

A few thoughts about the question first. It is possible the topic was chosen at random from the story just to see how David communicates. But it is more probable that the interviewer has asked the question because he or she is personally interested in the topic or they use spreadsheets a lot at work. So you want to say that you know all about spreadsheets. If you do then great – let them have it. If you don't really have a deep background in this topic then say what you have done and say that you are interested in it and would like to learn more. Good employees either know all the necessary technical skills or are eager to learn them – either one is fine for a new recruit.

Let's assume that David has done a small amount of spreadsheeting but is not an expert in the area.

David

'Well, I did the one for the Crows Nest Crab Company and I have done a few financial models in the accountancy course. Mostly discounted cash flow and that sort of thing. I'd like to have the chance to get a bit more experience with spreadsheets. Do you use them a lot here?'

Here David has given a short answer, because he knows he will get himself into trouble if he tries to appear to be a real expert. But, he recognised what was going on and gave two really good counter points to lead the interviewer away from his lack of expertise. He made up for a potential lack of ability with a plus point on motivation. He said he would like to have the chance to get more experience – now the interviewer knows that he can admit when he needs to ask for help or needs to learn more. This is a crucial area for all successful employees.

Then he asked if spreadsheets are used a lot at Taylor and Long. This is a really good end to the answer. It shows more interest and it lets the interviewer have a chance to talk about spreadsheets. People generally prefer to talk about their favourite topics rather than listen. It is good even when you are being interviewed to show that you are a good listener.

You should be able to see by now that experience stories are a bit of a cat and mouse game with the interviewer. You can play the game much better if you have spent the time before the interview to prepare your material. As you go through this section of the book, slow down a bit and try to put yourself in David's position and then in the position of the interviewer. Think about what is going on in each person's mind.

We will use a non-technical or soft skills question for the next example.

Interviewer

'You mentioned in your CV that the team you were in all got on well together. Do you think this is very important in the workplace?'

Again, a few thoughts about the question before we get to the answer. This is obviously a *fit* question, with the opportunity to bring in motivation. Almost every job these days involves teams or quite a few interfaces with other people. Even if you don't genuinely like working in teams, your answer to this question is that you think teams are important and you like working in them. It's all right to say that you can work hard on your own and can be independent when you need to be, but don't say that you dislike teams. And don't forget teams are usually made up of one leader and many followers – you definitely need to show that you can follow as well as lead, especially in your first few years of work.

So on to the answer.

David

'Yes I think they are really important. I think that almost all work these days involves other people and we have to be able to get on well together. It's so much more fun to be together when the team works and that makes it a lot easier to work well.

I concentrated on this quite hard with the hockey team at University. At first a few of the players didn't get on too well. We had two guys who both wanted to play on the left wing and there was quite a bit of friction. I said they could alternate between left back and left wing every other game. Things were a bit stilted at first but now they get on well. They often change positions in the middle of a game now, and sometimes actually switch in mid-play if it looks like it might give us an advantage.'

In this answer David brought a lot of good points in to the interview. Teamwork is essential in almost any workplace, but it's not really that important in school or university. Every professional has to make a transition from going it alone and competing against everyone else in school to working in teams and helping each other at work. Interviewers are looking to see if their applicant is a mature team player. David confirmed that he thinks good teamwork is important in the first part of the answer, and then gave a nice example of how he actually created teamwork out of a potentially difficult situation in the University second hockey team.

An employer doesn't really care if you played for the first or the seventh hockey team – they care about what skills you learned there that you could transfer to the workplace. David showed that he learned about how to motivate people in teams and not just about how to put a penalty into the top corner.

For a second example of an experience story for David, let's take a different topic, his grades at University. Grades are telling of an applicant's ability and motivation. David's grades are all right, but not stunning. It would be wise for him to have a story ready to explain why he got a 2.2 not a first or 2.1 in his second year exams in case they ask, or even if they don't ask, you can slip this kind of story in when you get the chance. Employers prefer 2.1s to 2.2s – that doesn't mean it's a huge problem; it just means you need a story.

Interviewer

'David, you got a 2.2 in your exams, do you think you will get a 2.1 in your finals?'

David

'Yes, I think I played a bit too much hockey last year and being captain was more work than I thought it would be. But still I

couldn't ignore the responsibility, so I worked as much as I could. I think I will have a bit more time to study next year.'

David has countered the problem of his 2.2 grade nicely. The truth is he probably spent a bit too much time in the bar last year, but he produces a reasonably convincing story, again that offers a solution and not just an excuse.

You could take a few minutes now to have a look through your CV and imagine the sort of stories that you would need to come up with in an interview. If you don't have a CV yet, then now is a good time to have a first go at one. Use the structure given on page 117-8. We have already suggested that you make a few rough notes; try to fill in your experience with some more detail now.

There are other points to consider when writing your CV. The next chapter uses the basis of the experience stories and shows you how to produce a first rate professional CV.

Chapter eighteen summary

☑ **A good story is a tactful way to describe your strongest points to the interviewer with proof that what you are saying is real. It is much more powerful than just saying 'I'm this, I'm that and I'm the other.' And what's more you can link your stories directly to their world by using buzzwords from their industry.**

☑ **You can make the interview very much easier for yourself by priming your CV with buzzwords that relate to your stories.**

☑ **Most interviewers don't want to ask a lot of difficult questions, they want to get to know you and to see what you have done.**

☑ **You can have a major influence on the content of your interview if you develop good stories that relate to the**

research you did on the industry and prime your CV with the right buzzwords. You can show the interviewer your ability, motivation and fit without him or her having to grill you for it.

- ☑ **You should be able to see a bit more clearly now how to put these stories together.**

- ☑ **Find the right buzzwords and then tailor your experience to be as close as possible to what the interviewer wants to hear. You don't have to be an expert in their field, but you do need to know the basics.**

- ☑ **Offer solutions not problems, show that you have energy, and show that you want to learn.**

19

CVs in More Detail

We have looked at CVs and experience stories in the previous section – here we will go into a little more detail about how to write the CV itself.

Below is a standard format for a CV. It is the same one that was used for David's CV in the previous section. You can adjust the format, or use your own format if you like as long as the CV remains clear, well spaced and easy to read. MS Word has some easy to use CV templates. Keep it business-like – no clip art, gimmicks, jokes etc. The CV below has notes in it to explain the purpose of each section.

Curriculum Vitae
Your Name

Job objective	You need to include a job objective. State specifically which job you are looking for. Then the reader knows you are a genuine candidate for their position and not a time waster. Make this section stand out. Use bold, or a border.
Education and experience summary	This is a two or three liner to identify you. It is an introduction. The interviewer can read it in just a few seconds. When someone is reducing 100 CVs down to 20 to study more closely he or she will only read the job objective and your summary. If you don't have a summary, your CV could go straight to

	the bin even if you are a very good candidate. Make this section stand out with bold font or a border.
Work experience **Company name** **Date from, to**	Two or three lines describing what you have done. Include buzzwords from your experience and research. This is the invitation for your experience story. Use holiday work, university or school projects if you have not worked before. It is all relevant, but link it as much as you can to the buzzwords of the job. Include hints towards ability, motivation and fit.
Company name **Date from, to**	
Education	
Name of establishment	Subject(s)Exams taken with grades (or without grades if they are very bad).
Name of establishment	Subject(s)Exams taken with grades (or without grades if they are very bad).
Societies, sports and organisations attended	Include all that you can here. It does not have to be business related. You want to show that you have energy and initiative to do more than the minimum required to get through school or university. It is essential that you show motivation and fit. If you don't have anything to include here then think about joining an organisation or club fast. Show teamwork where possible. Say you enjoyed yourself even if you didn't.

Other interests, languages, PC and other IT skills etc.	As above, you want to show that you have the energy to do more than the minimum to get through life. Languages and IT skills are both very important.
Contact Details	
Address	
Phone	Hard line and mobile if possible
Email	

There are two overall types of CV. The historical CV (as above) and the functional CV. The historical CV presents your past in the order that it happened (reverse order usually) with dates for everything that you did. The functional CV doesn't include dates and describes things that you did rather than actual job titles. It is much less specific. We advise against using a functional CV.

There is only one reason why people write functional CVs and that is to cover things up. So, the first thing the recruitment person has to do is to find out what you are covering up. From their point of view, it could be absolutely anything and they have to find out. You end up telling them anyway if you do get an interview, but a lot of functional CVs just get binned straight away. Why spend time on someone who is obviously covering something up when you have 80 others in the pile who are not? If you have a gap that you have to deal with, then face up to it and produce a convincing story.

The art of a good CV is to provide interesting, believable content. Give the interviewer what he or she wants to read. That doesn't mean you can make things up, but there can be many different ways to present your experience and education. That's what the experience stories are all about – presenting your experience in the best light possible for a particular job.

Here is an example from my own career.

After five years in the oil and chemicals business I went back to university to do an MBA. The MBA school put together a book of all the students' CVs and sent it out to hundreds of companies who might be looking for MBA graduates.

I had a lot of good experience and wrote it all down in my CV. I asked the careers advisor to review it. Her first comment when I went to ask her opinion surprised me a bit. She said,

'Why are you doing an MBA when you want to be an engineer?'

I replied,

'What? That's the last thing I want to do. Who told you I want to carry on in engineering?'

She said,

'You did – it's all you wrote about in your CV. Do you think a management consultancy firm cares about new ways of making styrene?'

I was proud of my technical achievements and eager to talk about them, but as she pointed out, the type of employer I wanted to work for wouldn't want to hear about styrene. They wanted to hear about management experience, teamwork, impressing people (especially clients), running workshops and so on.

So, I completely re-wrote my CV taking out all the technical information and replacing it with skills I had learned that were transferable to the new industry. And I was invited to lots of interviews and, with a bit or work on interview technique, I found the job that I wanted in management consultancy.

We have mentioned before that experience does not have to be work experience. Most people don't have much, if any, work experience when they apply for their first full-time job. You can draw on almost anything that you have done if you can identify skills or experiences that may be relevant to the position that you want.

General dos and don'ts in your CV

- Do write a new CV for every different job. General CVs are boring to the reader. As we keep saying, it's a lot of work, but worth it.

- Try to avoid starting every sentence with 'I'. (I did this ..., I did that ...).
- Don't include middle names and definitely no nicknames. Your forename and surname are perfectly adequate. Maybe your interviewers don't like long double-barrelled middle names – don't give them the chance to reject you on irrelevant grounds.
- Photographs – we advise against including a photograph unless the application form specifically asks for one. You want to be judged on your qualifications and experience, not your eyebrows.
- Date of birth – again we advise against including it unless it is specifically asked for. You might just disqualify yourself on the basis of age before the reader has had a chance to see what a good applicant you are in the rest of your CV.
- Do give specific dates of your activities and make sure there are no gaps. If you have a period of time where you did not do anything for a long time you should be prepared to be asked about it. You can say you were taking a holiday or a year out – that's okay. Employers can be suspicious of gaps. An applicant could have been fired and unable to get a job for a long time (not a good sign) or could have been in jail or had a long-term illness that might affect his or her future employability. Most companies run employment checks to make sure that all the names and dates of education and employment history tie up. Don't try to fool them. The bottom line is that if you have a gap, then you need a story to explain around it.
- Don't use an unusual font, Times New Roman, Courier or Arial are fine.
- Do try to include something that will set you apart from the other candidates. For example, my brother collects snakes (which my mother and I both think is rather unusual!). He always includes this on CVs and people always ask him about it. It's not relevant to his job at all – he's a lawyer – but it makes his CV easier to remember.

Exaggeration and embellishment in CVs

We all want to appear to be as good as possible in our CVs. However, you can't just 'invent' experience. The business world is surprisingly small in terms of bad reputations; don't get one. So, there is a fine line between what is good presentation and what is fiction.

Here is a quick example from David's CV. In one of his summer jobs in the accounting firm he actually spent a lot of time doing photocopying and making coffee. He wrote on his CV that he was working in the tax department and helping the team to keep going in late night work sessions. That's fine. What would not be fine would be for him to say he was providing the tax advice for that particular client.

I knew people when I was doing my MBA who did make things up in their CVs, studied the areas they made up, bluffed the interview and got the job. Some of them found themselves way out of their depth and left the job as soon as they could, but a few got away with it. It's risky and unethical, but some people do it.

How to deal with a failure or weak point in your CV

Many of us have at least one difficult area of our history that we might have to deal with in interviews. For example:

- bad grades or failures in examinations
- having been fired from a previous job or thrown out of university
- having been unemployed for a long period of time.

If you don't have to put a failure in your CV, then don't. For example, if you passed seven O levels and failed two you can just include the ones you passed. If the interviewer asks if you failed any in the interview then you need to be honest but if they don't ask then you don't have to tell.

If you passed but are not proud of your grades then, again, you don't have to put them in. If the interviewer is interested in exams then he or she will probably ask and you will have to be honest.

A good friend of mine had a third for his University degree, but he wanted to be a management consultant. Generally, consulting firms never take on employees who got thirds at University. He was rejected by very many because of this third, so he omitted the grades from his degree in his CV. One firm simply did not ask. So he did not have to answer. He got the job, has been regularly promoted since and is enjoying a very successful career as a management consultant now. It was a tough route for him and he had to suffer many rejections on the way, but he did achieve his goal.

When you have a weak area in your CV, the important thing is to have a story ready. You want to be able to show that you know why you did badly and how you will avoid this sort of performance in the future.

Personal computer skills

Almost all jobs these days involve work on a computer. General PC skills and specifically Microsoft Office (Word, Excel, Access, PowerPoint, and Outlook) are essential in many jobs. IT users can be described in three categories:

- don't know much about it, can't really use it
- can use it happily when you need to but don't concentrate on learning all the details
- power user – you have a lot of experience with the program and can help other people when they get stuck.

If you are a power user, then definitely include this on your CV. Whatever job you want, this is a big plus for you. Many of today's managers left school or university before PC skills were taught formally. They have picked up how to use the programs as they went along and are not always that proficient. You can be a big help on day one of your first job if you know these programs well. There is also a tendency nowadays to employ fewer secretaries and for individuals to do more tapping of the keys themselves. The higher your PC skills, the better.

If you are in the second category, then you should also put this on your CV if it is your first full-time job. Most applicants will be happy using the PC, but not all.

If you are not at all familiar with PCs and MS Office you should learn as soon as possible. If you have to admit in an interview that you don't know how to use at least MS Word and Outlook (or other word processor and email programs) your interviewer will not be impressed.

Objectivity and subjectivity

Some applicants are tempted to give very rosy descriptions of themselves in CVs or applications. For example, *'I am a highly motivated team player who has the ability to fit in wherever needed.'*

Put yourself in the interviewer's position when he or she reads this. Applicants can write anything on their CVs. These types of sentences are completely subjective and unproven to the reader. He or she needs proof and examples. We suggest that you don't write any sentences that are merely descriptions of yourself. Use stories of what you have done to tell the reader what sort of person you are. You can include the same points, you just present them in a way that shows it's real. Keep it objective.

There have been quite a few books written in the past on letters and interviews that use this style of self description. It is more acceptable in the USA than in the UK. If you are applying in the UK then beware if you have read US published books that advise you to go along and say, *'Well, good morning, I'm a motivated, team oriented, successful potential employee, and it's nice to meet you.'*

Proofing and checking

It is essential that there are no mistakes in your CV, or in anything else that you send in an application. Check it a few times and definitely get someone else to read through before you send it. It's easy to miss your own mistakes even when you read through it three or four times. Mistakes look absalutely teribbble.

Cover letters

There have been entire books written on how to write a good cover letter. Inside experience from the recruitment business suggests they are not as important as they may seem. Often a recruiter will only read the first couple of sentences of the cover letter, if anything at all. Put yourself in the recruiter's position. He or she might receive a hundred applications for one or two positions and will narrow down 100 CVs to around 20 in an hour or less. That's under a minute per CV. The recruiter will usually look at your job objective, your experience summary and your qualifications. It's pretty boring work as well so don't make the recruiter's life difficult by writing pages of blurb that they have to sift through to get to the crunch points. After narrowing down the CVs, the recruiter will read the 20 in more detail and select between five and ten to invite for interview. Even when studying the CV in more detail, recruiters often don't go back to read the cover letter.

You do have to write a cover letter, but keep it short and to the point. Put your ammunition in the CV, not the cover letter.

The letter should state clearly which job you are applying for and should include a very brief experience summary (two or three lines). This summary should include your most important qualification for the job.

If you have found this vacancy through a contact whom the recruiter knows, then mention the name in the cover letter right at the top – a personal contact sets you apart from the other applicants. (Better still, get the contact to phone the recruiter to tell him or her what a wonderful chap or gal you are).

Keep the letter formal. Check that you have the names all spelled correctly and get someone else to proof read it before you send it. As with the CV, mistakes may cost you the opportunity to get an interview.

Here is an example cover letter that you can use.

May 12 200X

Your address

Mr Fred Thomas
Director of Personnel
Bates Ltd
15 Grove Rd
Knittingham
Surrey, S11 111

Dear Mr Thomas

I am writing in response to your advertisement for trainee computer network specialists that was in the Times recently. I am hoping to become a network specialist and would be very interested to come to talk to you about the position.

I am currently studying computer sciences at Mannton Technical College, and am specialising in networks. I have also taken time on my own to read up as much as possible on Novell's networks that seem to be very innovative.

Please find my CV and contact details enclosed.

I look forward very much to hearing from you.

Yours sincerely

Janet Tanner
Tel: 01234 56789
Email: JT@Jnet

Company specific application forms

Some firms still insist that you fill out their own application forms. They have a set of written questions that they have used for probably quite some time and it makes life easier for them if all the applicants answer the same questions.

All the same principles apply to these application forms as to your experience stories and your CV. Do your research, find out about the key areas for the firm, find out some key words and write the answers to the application questions using your experience stories as usual.

Some firms may still ask you to fill out the forms by hand. In previous years hand writing experts were used to try to infer the characteristics of the applicants from their writing. Hand writing experts are used much less these days – it was all a bit like reading the tea leaves or the crystal ball. However, if you fill out a form by hand it must be neat and have no mistakes. Photocopy the form and write the whole thing out longhand on the copy in pencil. Check it, proof it and play with the words on the copy(s). When you are completely finished on the copies, transcribe it onto the original form. Hand writing analysis is more popular on the continent than in the UK or the USA.

(Personally I would think twice about applying to a firm that still asks for a handwritten form – it is a very out of date method, so it is probably an out of date firm, and that is not good for a new recruit).

References

Most employers will ask for one or two references from previous employers, school or university. Almost always they are confidential – you are not allowed to see what is in the reference. The firm wants to see from an independent source whether your experience is broadly true and what sort of person you are.

The main influence that you do have on the content of your reference is if you can choose whom to ask. This can be very important. With references from a previous job, ask someone who you are sure, or at least pretty sure, liked you. The reader of the reference will probably not know the internal structure of your last employer so will probably not be too suspicious if the reference did not come from your last direct boss. As long as the referee had a visibly higher position in the firm than you that should suffice.

There are some unethical ways of getting around the secrecy of references. Some people have asked referees for one more references than they actually need and arranged for it to be sent to a shadow address where they can pick it up. My personal opinion is that it's a pretty low thing to do, but people have done it. If the reference is terrible then they get someone else to do them all again.

Getting it all in the post, and following up

When you have all your documents finished, print them all on good quality paper and make sure everything looks nice and professional. No old ink cartridges or coffee spots.

If a firm asks you to apply by email then that's fine, but your letter and CV must be on a smart looking attachment (usually MS Word) and not just as plain email text.

Keep an organised file with copies of everything you send. When you are applying to a number of firms at once, it can be hard to remember exactly what you have sent to whom.

Most firms will send an acknowledgement slip to say that they have received your CV and are reviewing it. If they don't, then wait a week and make a polite phone call to see if they received your CV. Applications can get lost or can be directed to the wrong person quite often. Keep phoning once a week or so until you have an interview, a rejection or they say that they are reviewing your CV and need a little more time. Some firms may bin your CV without replying to you and you need to know where you stand on each application.

If you are not invited to interview, then you absolutely must phone and ask why not. You're not trying to persuade them to change their mind – they won't – but you need to know why they did not select you. A rejection is an opportunity to learn important points that could lead you to land the next one. Don't waste it.

Don't worry about feeling a bit sorry for yourself if you get the big

NO. It's natural and everyone goes through it. When I'm in a situation like that, I say to myself that I can be miserable for one evening. Play Metallica, get a greasy takeaway and drink cheap booze – or whatever your thing is. But the next morning it's time for a Red Bull and a paracetamol. Wake up and get on with the next application. Life is too short to sit around for days worrying about something that didn't happen. Learn from it and go out and chase the next one. The next one could be the one that works out for you. **Go and get it.**

Chapter nineteen summary

☑ **Write a specific CV for each job and prime it with invitations for the interviewer to ask you for your experience stories. That gives you a degree of control over the content of the interview, which is a huge advantage for you compared to the other applicants.**

☑ **Write a historical CV and prepare a story for any difficult areas. If there is an obvious gap or omission you will be asked about it.**

☑ **Make sure you hint at the three areas, ability, motivation and fit, in your CV.**

☑ **Do include a cover letter but keep it brief. Include anything important in the first sentence or paragraph.**

☑ **Check the CV and cover letter and have someone else check them before you send them out. A mistake could cost you an interview.**

☑ **Always follow up an application if you have not heard anything for a week or longer.**

☑ **If you receive a rejection, phone up to ask why. You might learn a key point that helps you land the next job.**

Next ➔➔

This is the crunch chapter – the interview. Take time to think about how to put your best foot forward in the interview.

20

Interviews

Introduction

Your objective in reading this chapter should not be to learn a number of interview answers off by heart. It should be to learn how to develop your own answers. There are simply too many possible questions to try to learn all the answers, and even if you could, you end up with someone else's answers and not your own. A good interviewer can spot that a mile away.

We are going to look at how to develop answers and then go through a number of questions. Example answers are only provided for some of the questions. Bullet points to help your thinking are included for others. This isn't laziness on the part of the author, it's a deliberate ploy to help you to learn to develop your own answers. The more you practise developing answers, the better you will be, especially if you keep referring to what the interviewers are looking for and keep a balance between *ability, motivation* and *fit*. Remember to emphasise fit – this is the hardest area for employers to predict.

The interview is not a good time to start learning how to develop answers. Right now, on the other hand, probably is.

How to develop a good interview answer

Remember the points that the different interviewers are looking for.

The HR interviewer

- Do you have personal presentation and manner? (*fit*)
- Do you show maturity? (*fit*)
- Is there evidence that you can work hard? (*ability and motivation*)
- Do you have communication skills? (*ability and fit*)
- Is there evidence that you can work well in teams? (*fit)*
- Is this the right level of job for you – are you likely to be satisfied and stay with the firm? (*fit and motivation*)
- Is there evidence that you can fit into their particular company's culture? (*fit*)
- Are you helpful, happy and positive or negative or aggressive? (*fit*)
- Do they like you? (*fit*).

The department interviewer

- Does the applicant have the skills and/or qualifications to do the job? (*ability and motivation*)
- Can he or she use the qualifications? (*ability*)
- Does he or she have relevant work experience, and did he or she do well in it? (*ability, motivation and fit*)
- Is he or she a problem solver? (*ability*)
- Will he or she fit into the culture of this department? (*fit*)
- Do I like him or her? (*fit*)

Now here's a list of traits in applicants that they do not want. Many difficult questions are designed to lead you unaware into describing yourself in a negative way. We call it interview quicksand. The interviewer leads you to the quicksand and asks you to start walking. If you don't know what's going on you walk straight in and sink out of sight. If you do know what's going on, you walk around the quicksand with a nice quiet smile.

They want to know if you can be:

- lazy
- selfish

- egotistical or big headed
- unreliable
- hard to get on with
- a loner
- stubborn
- hare brained
- aggressive
- … this list could go on quite a long way.

Of course, you are none of these things, but you need keep on making that impression in the interview.

The interviewer's tactic is to pretend to be an agony aunt; he or she asks to hear about some of your problems. Then he or she rejects you because all you talked about was your problems.

Interviews aren't fair – but you know that now, so you won't be caught in the trap. Be prepared to walk around the quicksand, and not to sink into it in a fit of complaints.

Here are five points to remember when the question comes over the desk.

- Pause and think, don't say the first thing that comes to mind. If you didn't hear or understand the question ask for it to be repeated.

- Ask yourself, is there quicksand here? **Do not be negative**, even if the questions begs for it.

- Think about whether the question is probing for ability, motivation or fit, or some combination of the three. Make sure you answer the question itself and the sub-text of the question (ability, motivation or fit). Emphasise fit if you can.

- Have a mental flick through your experience stories, sometimes you can simply tell the story as is and sometimes you will have to modify it to answer the actual question. Your experience stories are your safe ground. You know there is no quicksand there. Use them or their modified forms whenever possible.

- If in doubt, keep your answer simple, stay out of trouble and look to score points on the next question.

Every time you develop a practice answer, go through these five points. That's the best way to get them lodged in your head. Try to develop enough practice answers that the five points spring to mind every time automatically.

Typical questions

Here are some typical questions. Some are answered for you so you can see how it's done. Think through answers for the rest. It's much better you learn to develop answers now than when you're in the hot seat.

1 Tell me about what you were doing at ?... (a section from your CV).

This is the cue for your experience story – let them have it. Remember to include lots of fit.

2 Tell me more about ...

This is the cue for a bit more detail from your experience story, probably centred around one of the buzzwords. You know what to do. Even if it's a technical question include fit if you can.

3 Why do you want to be a ...?

This question is very common in interviews for first jobs. There are no hidden agendas here. The interviewer wants to find out if you have a genuine interest in this line of work. It's a straight motivation question. Companies want to give jobs to people who are likely to stay with them for at least a few years. They don't want to take people who chose the job more or less at random and may not like it when they get there.

Find some genuine reason why you chose the job. You may be able to cover this with one of your experience stories or you can say that you have always been interested in it, you have talked to people in this line of work, a member of your family or a friend works in the industry and it has always attracted you.

Whatever reason you give make sure that you project genuine enthusiasm and you have researched the job and know what it entails. Don't just say that you think you like it but you don't know why. Find reasons and be ready to talk about them.

4 Why did you choose to apply to us?

This question is a bit trickier. The fact is you probably applied to this firm and most of its competitors and the truth may be that you don't really mind which one you go to. The interviewer probably knows this as well, but again he or she is looking to see if you have researched this company and if you know anything about it that you like. When doing your research, look for differences between this firm and the competition. You could say that the firm is more international than the competitors or the environmental reputation is better, or that the firm is a little smaller and you think that employees may be treated a little more as individuals than in the larger firms.

Many companies try to have some kind of advertisement or catchphrase to distinguish themselves from the competition. Find out what this is for your company. Often you can find a distinguishing quote in the Chairman's statement in the annual report.

5 What do you think about ... (recent news/politics item)?

I remember once I went to a two-day selection event for university sponsorship with ICI. They asked me what I though about the EEC butter mountain. I didn't think anything about the EEC butter mountain, and in fact I prefer margarine. They preferred the other candidates to me.

In the weeks (or months) before interviews you should watch the news, read the paper if you have time or at least read *The Economist* or some other weekly or monthly business/political summary magazine. If you really feel that you don't have time to do this, then as an absolute minimum ask your Mum or Dad, or a friend about what has been going on lately in the outside world.

Look specifically for any hot topics in the industry that you are applying for. If you are planning to enter the car industry and Ford is closing a big factory, you need to know about it to look competent. Search for recent news in your industry on the net, the BBC news service is a good place to start.

6 How did you enjoy working at XYZ (your summer job)?

Here are some thoughts to help you:

- You found it interesting because ... (*motivation*)
- You felt at home in your team because ... (*fit*)
- And you found your experience from your college project in ... invaluable (*ability*)

Try to develop your own answer here. We have included a bad answer so that you can see what to avoid. This is what you **don't** want to say;

'Actually it was OK, but I expected it to be a bit more interesting. The boss was really busy and he never had time for me. I spent most of the time answering the phone and doing filing. That's why I'm here, because it looked like a bit of a dead end there. You don't ask new recruits to do the filing do you?'

Think about push and pull. The wonderful job that you're interviewing for pulls you to this company. Don't appear to be pushed by all the awful other jobs and bosses you have come across.

7 Where do you see yourself in five years time?

- Here? (*motivation*)
- Doing whatever is one or two rungs up the ladder from the job you are applying for? (*motivation, ability and fit*)
- You could turn this into a question – how do you develop people from this job and what is a reasonable expectation for five years time? (*motivation*).

Develop an answer for yourself.

8 What do you think is the most important quality in an employee at work?

- Your words for, you guessed it, *ability, motivation* and *fit*! Emphasise fit.
- Try to link to an experience story where you can talk about all three.
- There is no right or wrong answer, just make sure you produce a logical well-reasoned answer.

9 How good are you on a PC?

We mentioned this in the chapter about CVs. If you are a power user make a point of it. If you are competent say it. If you don't know much about PCs learn now before you go to an interview. Very few companies will employ someone who has not spent the time to learn to use a PC.

10 Do you use the internet a great deal?

This question is a double-edged sword. You need to appear to be au fait with the net, but you may not want to give the impression that you live in chat rooms or other possibly 'interesting' sites on the net. Talk about business related internet research that you have done.

11 Are you mobile? Could you work in our regional offices or abroad?

It's best to be honest about this. If you are mobile, then great, but if you are not prepared to move, don't try to fool them. Companies that rely on mobility often have it written into the employment contract – it's a big risk to sign it and hope they don't ask you to move. If mobility is in the contract, and they ask you to move and you say no, then you have a serious problem. Not a good start to your career.

Difficult questions

We are back to interview quicksand again. The interviewer is probing to see if you have any less attractive character traits or past experiences. Don't be drawn in, go around the quicksand. Always try to get back to your experience stories if you can (be careful to answer the question though). If your story doesn't do that, then don't use it. If you feel you are becoming emotional (anger, fear or adrenaline) pause, take a breath and say to your self, 'it's just quicksand, and I know how to go around it.' Give a small, slow smile before you respond.

1 Tell me about a time you failed in something?

This question can be awkward if you are not prepared for it. It can also be a plus point for you if you deal with it well.

If there's evidence on your CV that you failed in something then the question is a dead cert. Be prepared for this question (or better, re-write your CV). The key to the answer here is not to pretend that you did not actually fail. The interviewer will not believe you. The key is to show that you understand what happened and have learned not to do it again.

It is not a crime to fail in things; the only people who have never failed are the ones who have never tried anything. It is better to fail on a point of distraction or in a minor point of ability than to fail on motivation or fit. A small piece of technical knowledge is easy to fix – you study the subject until you know enough. Problems of motivation and fit are more entwined with a person's character, which is unlikely to change a great deal.

An example could be if you failed your maths GCSE. Don't say that you didn't like the subject and you thought it was boring so you didn't bother trying, and don't say that you are simply no good at maths. Neither of these points will get you a job.

However, you can say that you were really interested in biology (as long as you passed it) and you spent too much time focused on the subject you enjoy without really realising that you neglected your maths. You could say also that you were playing for a soccer team and you did not want to let your team-mates down. You felt that they were really relying on you so you did not do as much revision as you should have. You realise that this was a mistake now and GCSEs are more important than soccer teams, but you realised it too late. You stopped playing serious soccer in the run up to your 'A' levels.

What you need to show is that you picked yourself up and kept on going. You need to show that you understand why you failed, that you have learned from the experience and it won't happen next time.

Even if you don't have an obvious failure on your CV, you may still be asked this question. This time you have the choice of the topic of the failure. Prepare a small experience story in advance that focuses on how you learned from the failure and how you would avoid it in the future.

2 Tell me what you think are your strengths and weaknesses?

This again can be a bit of a tricky question. It is hard to talk about your strengths without coming across as arrogant and you can dig a big hole for yourself with weaknesses.

Deal with weaknesses in a similar fashion to the question above on failure. Choose something that would not be particularly serious or detrimental to your performance in a job in the first place and talk as much as possible about how you have recognised this weakness and learned to deal with it or get along with it. **Remember that you are not weak on motivation or fit.**

An example could be that you find repetitive tasks a little less interesting than conceptual work. Note that you do not say that you can't do them; you just say that repetitive tasks are not your ideal work. You can say that you find it helpful to break up repetitive tasks with other more interesting work, or you try to get them done first thing in the day and you know that once they are out of the way the day will be fine. Either way you recognise the problem and describe a solution – that's what the interviewer needs to hear.

For strengths use the experience stories. Go back to your job research and try to find a strength of yours that can be associated with one of the buzzwords for the job. For example, a buzzword for accounting was 'detailed numerical work', so you could talk about spreadsheets that you have done or some other numerical work that you enjoyed.

When talking about strengths, try to be objective and use examples. Anyone can sit there and say, 'well I'm really good at this, that and the other.' That does not earn you any points. Talk about something you actually did – no one can argue with that. Say you really enjoy whatever it is and give an example where you showed that you were good at it, then the interviewer knows that what you say is real. Use an experience story if possible.

3 Tell me about a boss or teacher you really didn't get on with at all.

This is classic quicksand. Do not fall in. It is an invitation for you to be negative, show any problems that you have with authority and have a general moan. Employers are terrified of employing graduates who are good at exams, appear pleasant in the interview and then turn out to be awkward with the boss. Use the same approach as with all these questions – keep out of trouble and say something positive. Don't complain in an interview. You could simply say that haven't had a particular problem with any teacher or boss. Some interviewers may push you on this question, stick to your guns, you liked your bosses and teachers.

4 Tell me about a time you were under pressure and how you dealt with it.

- You should be able to use an experience story here.
- Working under pressure is often about problem solving, assess the problem, refer to your knowledge, solve the problem.
- Include teamwork if possible. Explain how you got on well together despite the pressure.

Here's an example of a terrible answer. Do not say anything like this.

'Well, we had a project to design a bridge at college. We were in teams of three. It was an easy project really but one person in the team kept getting it all wrong. I was telling him that it was wrong but he wouldn't listen. Really stubborn, you know what I mean. The other person wasn't that much help either so I ended up doing it all night just before we had to hand it in. Of course, I got it done but it was a lot of pressure. Next time I'd just do it on my own to start with.'

This candidate proved he couldn't work in teams. It doesn't matter how good or bad the other two were. Develop an answer for yourself that proves you can.

5 Do you prefer to work in teams or alone?

- You know this answer by now. You love teams, but you can go it alone when you have to.
- You could give a short team based experience story to back up your assertion.

6 What would you do if your boss was being completely unreasonable?

- You would try to understand why.
- You might ask a co-worker what he or she thinks.
- You would not get emotional or angry.

Read chapter 22 on 'Getting on with the boss' and then run through your own answer.

7 Tell me what you really don't like doing.

The only thing you really don't like is falling into quicksand that is as obvious as this one.

- Don't refer to anything work related.
- You could say you can't think of anything, or maybe the washing up.

8 What interests you least about this job?

More quicksand. Smile slowly and go around it. Develop your own answer now. You love this job because ...

Irrelevant questions

You may be asked some questions that strike you as completely irrelevant to the interview. Don't be shocked or annoyed. These can come from a bad interviewer who has nothing better to say or a trained professional who can interpret your answer clearly in terms of motivation or fit. Same as any other question, pause, think back to what the interviewer is looking for and develop an answer that shows fit, motivation (and ability if possible).

1 What would you do if you had a million pounds?

This is a *motivation* question.

- Don't say that you would spend the next fifty years getting a suntan.
- You might set up your own business in the same line of work as the firm you are applying to.

2 If you could meet anyone from history who would it be?

This question is designed to test your values. Who do you look up to? It is a *fit* question. You are trying to show fit with an organisation so choose someone who was famous for leading an organisation. Choose someone now, and develop an answer as to why you picked him or her.

3 What is the most important thing you have ever done?

Go back to *ability, motivation* and *fit.* Choose something that emphasises one or two of them. Try to find something that was in an organisation and involves other people.

Think through an answer now.

4 What do you think of the current Prime Minister?

The quicksand is back again. If a candidate slates the PM then he or she could also slate the Managing Director of the firm. You can disagree with a policy but don't express dislike for the person.

Think through an answer.

5 What were the last three books that you read?

A skilled interviewer might try to interpret your character by what you read. But he or she would probably get it wrong. Go back to basics. Ability, motivation and fit. Choose books that show some interest in each. Quote one or two business books if you can. (Or you could just keep it simple and tell him or her the last three books that you read).

Illegal questions

Employers are not allowed to discriminate on the basis of age, sex, race, health, religion or how many children you have or want unless the issue has a genuine effect on your ability to do the job. They are not allowed to ask questions that are designed to test these issues without good reason that the answer will affect your ability to do the job. A dance company who needs a lead female dancer is allowed to rule out men, a bank that needs a bank clerk is not.

Illegal questions are difficult to handle but they are also quite rare. Almost all large employers know the rules, but there may be some small firms out there who don't. Our advice is to ignore the illegality and answer the question as best you can. Go around it if you find it too offensive. Get the offer and then choose not to take it if you don't want it. Losing your cool or telling the interviewer that he is asking illegal questions probably will not get you the offer. Offers are like credit cards – if you don't have one they're hard to get but once you have one you can get others more easily.

Nasty questions

Some interviewers take a pleasure in seeing you squirm. Not many, but they do exist, and other interviewers want to see if they can penetrate your calm composure by asking 'nasty' questions. The key to these questions is damage limitation. Don't say anything harsh, negative or arrogant. It can be difficult to find a brilliant answer to a nasty question that will secure the job offer for you. But, it is very easy to be led outside your experience stories and to forget ability, motivation and fit to say something that does not impress the interviewer. For these questions keep it simple, keep it positive and nice and keep out of trouble. If you get a nasty one, remember the golden rule; pause, and don't react emotionally. If they didn't think you were a good candidate they would not have bothered to interview you. A nasty question is just another test. It is not any kind of judgement about you, even if it appears to be exactly that. Don't take it personally. Go back to the basics and develop an answer based on ability, motivation or fit. Use an experience story if you can.

1 Why should I employ you?

Relax, and take him or her through a relevant experience story that shows ability, motivation and fit.

2 What is your impression of yourself?

Go back to *ability, motivation* and *fit*. Use examples to demonstrate how you might view yourself, rather than descriptions. Use an experience story.

This is a particularly nasty question so here is an example to help you. Don't try to learn it – think through an answer that is suitable for you.

'My impression of myself is that I try to analyse each situation for what it is and to be as helpful as I can depending on what is required. I remember in my summer job at Sainsbury's I was stocking shelves one minute, and then on the phone in customer service the next. They

were completely different jobs and I tried to look at what each one required and did as well as I could. I suppose that could mean my impression is that I try to be flexible.'

That is a *fit* answer. The point is the candidate can fit in wherever he or she needs to. You could produce a motivation or ability answer if you prefer. Just make sure you remain positive without being big headed and use an experience story to hint at your good impression of yourself rather than saying it directly.

3 What would you say if I told you that you're not doing very well in this interview?

This is a horrible question. We have never heard of it actually coming up in an interview. Don't expect interviews to be this bad. But if you are prepared for the worst then you will find all the other questions easier.

Here's a bad answer. *'Well why are you still asking me questions then?'* This candidate ran into the quicksand eyes shut. The interviewer is trying to see if he or she can make you angry.

A better answer would be, pause, breathe and say *'I would assume you are trying to see how I respond to being under stress'.*

Try to come up with something else yourself. Concentrate on fit, people who get ruffled easily often don't fit into the culture of the firm.

4 Do you really think you are good enough for this job?

Relax, and take him or her through a relevant experience story that shows ability motivation and fit. Don't just sit there and say 'Yes.'

You should have the right idea about nasty questions now. Don't think of them as nasty, don't become emotionally involved, walk around the quicksand and give a positive answer that involves ability, motivation or fit, just as you would for any other type of question.

There are other interview questions that you may be asked. In this section we have shown you how to think about the question before you answer, how to play the interview cat and mouse game instead of just saying the first thing that comes into your mind. Few interviews contain more than one difficult question, and quite often there won't be any at all. You are better off to spend most of your time making sure that your 'meat and potatoes' answers are really good rather than trying to anticipate every single tortuous question that has ever come up.

However if you still feel worried by difficult questions, there are books that provide a larger number of answers. A suggestion is *'Great Answers to Tough Interview Questions'* by Martin John Yate. But don't just try to learn someone else's answers off by heart; there are simply too many possible questions that might come up. You can't remember answers to all of them. Learn how to play the interview game.

Questions for you to ask the interviewer

You should go to each interview with four or five well thought out questions. The purpose of these questions is not really for you to find out new information; it is to show that you are interested in the company and in the interviewer. The questions should be designed to manage the impression that you make in the interview.

Try to ask open-ended questions – questions that need a full answer, not just a yes or no. Generally people like to talk more than they like to listen and your interviewer has just spent most of the interview listening. You can now show what a great communicator you are by asking something that needs a bit of explanation. You can show what a good listener you are.

For example you could ask; *'Could you explain the training and career development programme that you have for new recruits?'* That's an open-ended question that shows motivation. The interviewer can talk for as long as he or she wants to.

The closed-ended equivalent would be *'Do you have a training and career development programme for new recruits?'* This question could invite a yes or no answer, which is not what you want.

Try to prepare five questions. You're only going to ask two or three but quite often the questions can already have been answered by the conversation in the interview, so you need a couple of back-ups.

Remember ability, motivation and fit. Make sure you cover all three somewhere in your questions.

Here are some example questions that you can ask:

- As above – 'Do you have a training and career development programme for new recruits?' (*ability and motivation*)
- 'Do you pay specific attention to team work here at (XYZ), do you train people on team work?' (*motivation and fit*)
- 'Is there a broad range of future career opportunities within the firm for someone starting in this position?' (*motivation*)
- 'Could you tell me about the (XYZ) technology that you use here?' (You should have identified technology used in your research) (ability)
- 'Is the firm growing at the moment? Are there plans for future growth?' (motivation)
- Other technical questions based on your knowledge or research.

Feel free to come up with your own questions but always bear in mind that the purpose of the questions is to impress the interviewer rather than find out things that you should already know. If the interviewer showed what his or her pet topics are in the interview then ask about them.

Here are some questions you shouldn't ask:

- Questions about salary, benefits and holiday. Phone HR after you receive an offer to talk about the hard stuff.
- 'What hours do people work?' You look as if you don't want to work hard.
- Basic questions about the firm or industry that you should have covered in your research.

The panel interview

Most interviews are one-to-one, but you may be faced with two or three people on the other side of the table. Conduct yourself just as you would for a one-to-one interview, except remember to make eye contact with everyone on the panel and not just whoever is asking the questions.

Personal presentation and body language

First impressions do last and the first impression is made up substantially by how you appear. You don't need to be a fashion model to get a job, far from it actually. But you need to be dressed appropriately and you need to sit, stand, smile and greet in a positive way.

It's very easy to forget this when you're nervous and concentrating on all of the great material that you have prepared to impress the interviewer. If you wear an old looking suit, you scowl, hunch your shoulders, wring your hands and look at the wall, he or she will not form a good first impression.

Here is a true example from my own job searching experience. A friend and I were both looking for jobs after our MBA. We had both done very well in the course and exams. We were being invited to every interview available from the top firms, but we were not getting past the first round. We had no idea why. We studied our cases, practised our presentations and ironed our shirts like crazy, but to no avail. I asked my girlfriend what she thought. You won't believe what she said.

'Well have a lie in tomorrow and get up just in time for the Teletubbies. Set the video to record it. Watch it the first time through and then rewind it and the second time try to dance around and smile and laugh and talk in baby talk and pretend it's all very funny. Then stop and do a practise interview presentation'.

Our problem was that we were so full of Porter's five forces, Boston boxes and economic theory that we had forgotten to smile, to be nice, to be fun to meet. We were bent over squinting at our case study notes instead of catching the interviewers eye and giving a smile. I got the next job I went for, and my friend got one soon after that. This is really a true story – I had two degrees from Cambridge, six years international business experience and an MBA from Britain's top business school. It took a morning prancing around the living room to a Teletubbies video to land a job.

So let's talk about personal presentation and body language.

Body language

Some people naturally carry themselves in a confident manner and others don't. The first thing you need to do is to get an impression of your own natural body language to see how much work you need to do.

Try to get a video of yourself answering some interview questions. If you look very stiff, always cross your arms and legs, change your position very often, sit hunched up or talk with your hand near your mouth, then you need to work on your posture, sitting position and body language. Practising questions and body language with a friend or coach is much better than trying to do it on your own, other people can be much more objective about how you come across.

Here are some tips about body language.

The greeting with the interviewer

Stand up straight, shoulders back, look him or her in the eyes, say *'Hello, nice to meet you'* and do it all with a warm smile. Don't grin like a Cheshire cat from the moment you see the interviewer. Stand up and let your smile develop slowly, to show that you are glad to meet him or her personally and not that you grin aimlessly at everyone. Shake hands for approximately three seconds with a firm but not hard grip. Follow the interviewer into the room and sit down where he or she indicates. Don't sit down before being asked. Don't come closer than a metre from the interviewer – that's personal space reserved for close family and lovers, not job applicants.

Be ready for the greeting wherever you are waiting – don't have three books, your bag and a newspaper on your lap and a cup of coffee in your hand. You will miss the prime greeting moment while you disentangle yourself from the mess.

Sitting position

In most interviews you have a desk or table between you and the interviewer, which is a much more comfortable situation than just sitting opposite each other. Sit up straight, with your feet underneath you. When people are nervous they tend to adopt defensive body postures. Crossed legs, crossed arms, wringing of the hands, hands between the legs, not enough eye contact. You want to look as comfortable and natural as possible and not too defensive.

Try not to cross your arms and legs. A good start position is knees together and hands on your thighs or forearms on the desk if it's close enough. People who are relaxed tend to take up more space. Don't overdo it, but take a little space.

Eye contact is important. It is natural for people to avoid eye contact when they are unsure of what they are saying or when they are lying. Look your interviewer in the eye as you make your points and tell you stories. (But don't hold each eye contact too long; it could be read as a challenge).

It's fine to use your hands when you talk. You portray energy and enthusiasm.

If there is no desk or table you will feel a bit more exposed. This can happen in a panel interview, when they can't fit the whole panel behind a desk. It is harder to maintain a confident calm body posture when you are in an upright chair on its own. You want to adopt the same posture as above except there is nowhere to put your hands. You can hold a file on one thigh if you like which gives you a little bit of shielding and somewhere to put at least one of your hands. Cross your legs if you must, but don't cross your arms. It looks too defensive and cold.

One last point for the men to remember, (this should go without saying, but), if your interviewer is a lady, don't look at her boobs. So many people still do this in the office, it is really obvious, and it loses you points extremely quickly.

Dress codes

There is a standard code of dress for all office job interviews. You make up your own mind about what to wear later, but for the interview it is better to follow the formal dress code.

Men

You need a dark suit. Dark grey, navy or black. No brown, green etc. A blazer or sports coat and trousers is not formal enough. The suit must fit. If it looks old or doesn't really fit you, then buy a new one.

Get one in the sales, and haggle the price down, you can always haggle in suit shops. You don't need to buy a particularly expensive suit, a budget one that fits is better than an expensive one that does not. It is worth paying a bit extra to get it altered to fit you. You should be able to get a decent suit for under £100 if you look around. Single breasted and double-breasted are both fine. Buy a traditional business suit, not a fashion suit. My first suit cost me just £50 in a sale and it was good enough to get me the job.

Have a couple of new white shirts. Again, traditional business shirts, nothing fancy. Get them dry-cleaned or iron them with starch. Always wash your shirt before each interview. If you are nervous, it's hot and your shirt isn't clean, you may not be exactly spring fresh at the end of a long journey and a few hours of interviews – not a good way to impress the interviewer.

Shoes – black leather lace-up dress shoes (with some polish). Nothing else. Brown is not formal enough. No moccasins or easy shoes.

Tie – nothing too crazy. Bright is fine but conservative is better than gaudy.

Hair – short back and sides, boring but effective. It's okay nowadays for guys with a little less hair to have a crew cut, but not if you are lucky enough to still have all your hair.

Lay off the aftershave and jewellery. It's a job, not a date.

If I have a really long journey I usually take it all with me in a suit carrier and change when I get there, (although I have ended up changing in some interesting places). I take deodorant with me too.

Women

Wear a ladies' business suit (skirt and jacket). You have a bit more freedom in the colour than the men, but it's always better to stay on the formal or conservative side (black, navy or grey) for interviews. The skirt should be knee length or longer.

White or light coloured business shirt. Not see through or low cut.

Natural colour tights or stockings, or none at all.

Dress shoes, without high heels.

Minimum jewellery and perfume.

Business-like hairstyle.

It may seem a bit expensive to buy a good outfit if you don't already have one, but it is worth it. You will need it anyway as soon as you start a job. Even if the company has informal dress codes you need a suit for client meetings and other formal occasions. Try hard to buy in a sale, you can get good clothes at big reductions.

Summary – interviews

- ☑ **Most interviewers are not trying to catch you out; they are trying to get to know you and find out about your experience. All they want to know is 'are you one of us?' Put most of your preparation into really good material for this central part of the interview.**

- ☑ **If you write your stories well and you know them, and your CV was well primed with invitations, then you will not have a problem. This is the part of the interview where you land the job; you win your points here.**

- ☑ **The key to tricky questions is to keep out of trouble. Don't lose your hard earned points by trying to be too clever answering a tricky question. See the quicksand coming and go around it.**

- ☑ **Stay positive and pleasant at all times. Never complain about anything in an interview.**

- ☑ **Pay attention to your personal presentation and body language. Your first impression does count.**

- ☑ **Try to do a practice interview before you do the real thing. A video camera or just a mirror can be very useful.**

- ☑ **If you are still very worried about your interviews, then consider going to an interview coach.**

Other situations you may come across in the interview process

The business game

Some interview processes involve business games. A group of between three and six applicants are set a task to perform together in a set period of time and the selectors look on to see how you behave and what you come up with.

The games are a good way of seeing what an applicant is really like (quite often better than an interview). However, they can be awkward as you are forced to work alongside the other applicants, who are essentially your competition for the job(s).

There are two areas to think about here:

- the business theory of the game itself
- the team interactions.

The game itself

It is possible to use nothing but common sense to solve a business game problem, or it is possible to use the latest cutting edge business theory. The choice is yours. If you want to read up on business theory look at *'Ace your case'* by Wet Feet Press, **www.wetfeet.com**. The more you know the better.

If you have an interview day or weekend that involves a business game, it's a good idea to read up if you have time. If you don't have time to read up, here are a few very brief fundamentals.

- Most businesses exist to make as much money (profit) as possible in an ethical manner for the shareholders.

- Don't take any risks that have a real chance of bankrupting the business (i.e. don't bet more money than you have).

- Business starts with the client or customer. Know what they want and you can usually get them to pay for it (this is essentially marketing).

- Know who your competition is. You need to do something better than them, i.e. sell a better product, sell a similar product at a cheaper price or advertise better.

- Accountants break businesses down into costs and revenues. If the revenue is steadily larger than the costs, you are making money.

These are a mere five bullet points when you could fill ten libraries with all the business books in the world. Read up further if you were not familiar with the points above.

The team interactions

Often the selectors are more interested in how you get on with the other people than in your specific knowledge in these games. Read Part three of this book before going to your interview and your business game, especially the section on teams and teamwork.

If you find you can take the lead of the group then go ahead. A clear effective leader will impress the selectors. You can try to take the lead of the group by saying very early in the game (the first 15 seconds), *'We could look at the problem in this way,'* and then you explain your idea.

Another slightly more subtle way to take the lead is to start with *'Why don't we get some ground rules established first?'* You invite everyone to contribute. This can work well as everyone has a chance to put their ideas forward and so get their stab at leadership. But actually they're the ideas workhorses following your lead. If there is a flip chart, see if you can get the pen and be the one who is making notes.

However, usually at least half the group will be trying to take the lead, and it can end up as a mess if everyone tries it at the same time. It does not impress the selectors if you are one of three people each trying to talk over the others to get the other poor two or three to do what you say.

This is the usual situation you will have. There is a very important point to remember here. Most people at work are followers not leaders. You can't have 400 senior managers in a firm and 20 workers. You can impress the selectors by showing your team skills by working alongside the others, or even following their lead, especially if the leadership battle is a mess. If they are slinging mud, you can look good if you duck and get on with something useful.

Even if you are not trying to lead the group, you should still try to suggest plans of action. Don't merely listen to the others' plans and criticise them or reword them. It looks much better if you come up with something rather than just to talk about someone else's idea. Be positive. Say things like:

☑ 'Yes, that sounds great, and perhaps as well we could think about ...'

That earns you many more points than saying;

☒ 'Well I don't think that's quite right because ...'

If you don't like someone in the group, do not show it, don't raise your voice, smile as often if you can. Use first names. Make a point to remember everyone's name before the game. People like hearing their own name and when you use it they will usually listen to you. Keep track of time. It is easy to let time slip by as people jockey for position.

The case study – written or oral

The case study is similar to the business game but without the teamwork. It is more a test of how you think, how much you know about business and how good your verbal or written communication skills are.

The key to a good case study is to use a business structure to break the question down into manageable parts, solve the parts and fit them back together again. Again, it is beyond the scope of this book to teach all about business structures. If you have a case study coming up it is worth spending some time to learn about the following:

- the Boston consultancy matrix (the most famous structure – but a bit clichéd now)
- Porter's five forces
- time, cost, quality triangle (for project management)
- the four Ps of marketing (Product, Price, Promotion and Place).

Again, a good book to read is *'Ace your case'* by Wet Feet Press, available over the internet, **www.wetfeet.com**.

Stand-up presentation

You may be asked to do a stand-up presentation for a job interview, and it can be the most nerve-wracking challenge that you might face.

But, don't worry – just as with all the rest of the interview process, good preparation can make a presentation much easier and much more successful.

The first problem with presentations is nerves. If you know you have really prepared the presentation carefully and rehearsed it many times over, then you can feel confident that you know your material well and that you can deliver. Also you know that you have probably done more preparation than the other applicants.

The second problem with presentations is that very often the audience does not actually know what the presenter is talking about. It is much harder to follow a train of thought by listening to it than by reading it. Many people don't take this on board and lose their audience very early on in the presentation. We have a presentation structure that you can use for any presentation. It is easy to deliver and easy to follow. Our strong advice is that you use it.

You may have heard people talking about KISS. We'll I'm sure you have, but perhaps not in this sense. It means Keep It Simple Stupid. Otherwise everyone gets lost. (Personally, I prefer to aim for KIS not KISS, for obvious reasons).

Here is the structure, and a few notes about how to use it. The presentation has nine sections as described in the table opposite.

The One Liner	This is a one liner to wake them up and make them listen! Find something really punchy.
Why should I listen?	Here you spend a short period of time explaining why your audience should listen. The subject must benefit them in some way for them to bother giving you their precious attention. Explain what is in it for them.
Who you are and notes	Introduce yourself and deal with details of the presentation, e.g. you are giving out the notes so they don't have to take any themselves.
Presentation contents page	You will have three (or maximum four) main points. Introduce them all before you start to talk about them. Put the titles of the main points on a sheet of A1 paper labelled as 1,2,3 etc and leave this visible for the audience throughout the presentation so they always know where you are.
Point 1	Here you talk about your first point. At the end lead into the second point. Go to the contents page and tell the audience you are moving onto the next point.
Point 2	Here you talk about your second point. At the end lead into the third point. Go to the contents and tell the audience you are moving onto the next point.
Point 3	Here you talk about your third point. At the end lead into the summary.
Summary	Summarise all the points to make sure they remember what you said.
Questions	Invite them to ask questions. If you can encourage a lively discussion at the end of a presentation you will standout over those who did not.

It was fashionable about ten years ago to use PowerPoint in business presentations. It is not very fashionable any more. In fact it's boring, especially as you have to dim the lights to be able to see the screen – and that just makes people want to have a ten minute nap. You want people to be awake – you want bright lights and lots of personal energy and enthusiasm, not dim lights and a PowerPoint screen that your selection panel has seen a thousand times before. They are hoping to employ you, not PowerPoint. Let them see you.

Stand straight, try not to cross you arms, look them in the eye every now and then, smile, don't read word for word from notes – learn it off by heart if you have to.

If I'm really nervous before a presentation, I go into the loo five minutes before it, look in the mirror and say, *'It's going to be great, I can do it, I'm the man,'* and then come out walking tall and smiling at everyone. It sounds pretty silly – but it helps. Make sure the interview panel are not in the cubicles before you try it.

The drink in the pub with the department

Sometimes your interviewer will ask you out for a drink or even dinner with other members of the firm. They might tell you that this is not part of the selection process. It is.

They are trying to see if you get on well with the other employees. Also they might want to see what you are like after a few beers. Even if they are all drinking like fishes, it is better for you to stay reasonably sober, and to keep your jokes more or less politically correct.

That might seem a bit boring, but if you are out for a drink with the employees, you have probably already got the job. The main decision maker will have decided that you are worthy of an offer. They just want to check that you are still nice when you are let loose in a social situation. You don't really need to gain any more points in the pub; you just need to make sure that you don't lose any. If someone tells the boss that you were rude or obnoxious that offer can be taken back faster than you can say, *'Oh s*** – I need to write my CV again!'*

The selection weekend

Some firms will ask you to attend a weekend event for interviews and other selection events. These will almost always consist of interviews, business games, written tests or case studies, and social events. We have covered all these things separately in this section. Just remember that you are on show one hundred percent of the time. If they say you are not being judged in the bar in the evening don't believe it. Even if they do not actually mean to judge you they will, it's human nature.

It is quite likely that one of the 'candidates' is in fact an insider-observer, so take care with all your interactions and activities.

Psychometric tests

You may be asked to take some kind of personality or aptitude test in the interview process. It's best to just get on with it and don't worry about it too much. It's not worth trying to fool one of these tests by ticking the answers that you think the selectors want. Be yourself and be proud of it. If you want to look further into these tests look at a book titled *'All About Psychological Tests and Assessment Centres'* by Jack Van Minden, Management Books 2000.

Part 2 Conclusion

It's time for you to stop reading and get your fingers on the keyboard (or get the pen on the paper). Don't assume that just because you have read through this section that you can now ace your interviews. Go through the section again as you research and choose your target companies. Look through the example CVs and experience stories as you prepare your own.

It can be a lot more fun if you do this with a friend who is also looking for a job – get together and talk through your experience stories as you write them. Have your friend read through the stories and listen to you presenting them. Interview each other – use a video camera if you can. The best preparation is to go through your material with an experienced interviewer or career consultant, but doing it with a friend is much better than going it alone. Sometimes it seems even harder or more embarrassing to go through a mock interview with someone that you know than it is to do the real thing. It is all good practice.

Remember the famous golfing quote. 'The more I practise the luckier I get.' So get your pen out and start getting lucky!

Part Three

Start Treading the Path to Success

Part 3 Introduction

Well done! You've landed your job and today's the first day. You've parked next to an important looking Jag in the car park and found the front door. What's next? There are hundreds of them all pouring into the office and they all know where they're going and what they're doing when they get there.

You might remember the book and TV series called 'A Hitchhiker's Guide to the Galaxy'. They said that you could get round the whole galaxy with just one phrase. 'Don't Panic!' Whether it's galaxies or offices, that's good advice.

Larger firms usually run an induction course for new recruits. It's like a guided tour of the company, the building and some of the people. These can be really helpful, especially as you can make friends quickly with the other recruits. Smaller firms often don't have induction courses but with a bit of luck someone nice will show you around.

Some firms don't have induction courses at all, and don't show you around. When I turned up for my first job after university, I arrived at 8:30 am. I thought they started at 9 and I wanted to be early. The first thing I heard was that I was an hour and a half late – they started at 7 am (which had been previously better known to me as the middle of the night). They also thought I should have arrived a week later so they didn't have anything prepared at all. They sat me down at a desk in the corner on my own and gave me a couple of magazines to read.

'Ummm, what a lovely warm welcome that was, I'm so glad I flew four thousand miles for that!' I thought to myself. However after a couple of hours of being scintillated by *'Hydrocarbon Processing'* magazine, a chap called Pete came along to have a chat.

That was fifteen years ago, he lives in Moscow now and I'm writing this in the South of France – but I'm off to Moscow soon to visit my old friend Pete. So even if your first day isn't terribly good, don't panic, keep your spirits up and be as friendly as you can to everyone.

This section of the book is a guide to help you start off on the right foot in your new job. You will come across lots of different situations and many new faces. Sometimes it will be very obvious what to do and sometimes it won't. If you pay attention to the points you're about to read, you will have a very good idea of how to behave and what to do wherever you find yourself.

You will find that the emphasis is more on how to fit in with everyone else and not on how you can stand out quickly. To have a really successful career, you do need to stand out and become a leader, but in the majority of cases it's best not to try it too early. This is how a very large Louisiana oilman once described the point to me early in my career: *'Listen up, ya prep school Limey, ya gotta find ya feet before ya can go around kickin' everyone's ass.'* He was right, even if he wasn't very eloquent. Have a look at the follow-up book *'Faster Promotion in 90 Minutes'* by Neil Thompson, Management Books 2000, when you feel that the time is right to stand out from the crowd.

Most of the points in this third section are not directed at how you can become an expert in the technology or specifics of your job. You need to learn your technical skills but to be really successful, all the other skills are just as important. Most employees don't pay anything like enough attention to them.

School and university teach us mainly how to study, write, and solve problems on our own. If your answer is right you get the points. If your answer is right and everyone else's is wrong you get even more points. We are taught to work alone and to compete against each other most of the time.

At work, things could not be more different. If your work is right and everyone else's is wrong, the firm goes bankrupt and you're on the street. To get on the fast track at work, you need to work well with others. Even though you may be competing with them for the next promotion or pay rise, you need to work together like bees making honey on a day-to-day basis. Make the other firms in your industry your competition, not your co-workers.

Here are the thirteen topics, one short chapter each.

21

The Rookie Year

The first year at a new company can be a difficult experience. It can also be an experience where potential high flyers begin to stand out from the others. These standouts can be given better assignments, better training and more attention than the other new recruits. You want to become one of them as quickly as possible.

It is tempting to think that to stand out quickly you need to be different and to suggest new ways of doing everything. Usually the opposite is true. The standouts are the recruits who mould themselves into 'company people' the most quickly (in the hours at work anyway). They concentrate on building a solid reputation for themselves that will be the bedrock of their future success.

How quickly can you learn the company culture? Your progression depends on the impression that you make on the existing bosses and employees. Some new recruits are viewed as mature, dependable and easy to work with early on. They learned the culture quickly. Others are viewed as immature and needing more time before they will be given any work that really matters. The first year is a testing period, a getting-to-know-you period.

This can be frustrating for new recruits. You come from school or college with your head full of education, new ideas and enthusiasm. You want to take on a big important assignment where you can show everyone how good you are. Then you get to do the photocopying. It can be a bit demoralising.

In school or college, you can afford to get things wrong sometimes. At work you can't. There are no marks for getting it almost right. Companies often don't give important work to people who they don't know very well, and until you have been there for a year or so, they might feel that they don't know you very well.

There are always quite a lot of relatively menial and boring tasks to do in offices. Someone has to do this work, and nowadays companies tend to employ fewer secretaries than a decade ago (to save on overhead costs). New recruits often end up doing this work. It can be copying, filing, taking minutes, arranging meeting rooms and so on. It is easy to feel that this work is below you and to become frustrated.

The best plan is to swallow hard and get on with it. Take this work on and do it well. Finish every task completely. Never leave things half done because they are boring. Check everything before you hand it over. If you are not sure exactly what to do then ask someone. If you can, ask a co-worker before you ask your boss. Use your time doing these tasks to get to know people and to learn about the culture.

Try to make friends with people in the company who have been there longer than you. If you spend all your time with the new recruits then that is exactly how people will view you – as a new recruit. (You don't want to ignore your new friends – that's not the point, just make sure you mix it up). See if the company has sports clubs or other societies. These are good places to make friends with people from all over the company.

Don't try to change anything in the firm until you have become part of it. A suggestion to change something from a seasoned employee can be received as a great idea. The same suggestion from a new recruit can be seen as a threat and as a lack of respect for the current systems and people in the firm. You have to learn the rules before you can break them.

Personal appearance

Appearances do matter – especially at work. You need people to have confidence in you. They don't automatically know how brilliant you are – you have to show them – and your personal appearance can help a great deal. Look at the successful and popular people at work. How do they dress and what sort of body language do they display?

Office space is very expensive, especially in the cities. One CEO quoted thirteen thousand pounds per year per desk in West London. These prices are forcing employers to use cubicles, open plan desking and even hot desking. When you are working in such close quarters, your personal hygiene and mannerisms are extremely important to your reputation. Coming into the office having slept off too many Vodka Red Bulls on your friend's sofa is not okay anymore. Neither are the after effects of a vindaloo that was a little bit too hot. Cracking your knuckles, tapping your pen or even scratching a lot would go unnoticed in your own office, but not in an open plan or a meeting room. After a hard day, look in the mirror and ask if you would like to be sitting next to yourself. Make sure the answer is always yes.

Chapter twenty-one summary

☑ **When you first join a firm you are an outsider.**

☑ **The first year is a 'getting-to-know-you period'.**

☑ **Become an insider before you try to change anything.**

☑ **Build up a good reputation.**

☑ **Don't worry if the work isn't quite as stimulating as you expected at first. It's a stage you go through and the better you do it the faster you will get something more interesting.**

Next ➔➔

We look at how to handle the most important relationship you have in the office – the one with your boss.

22

Getting On with the Boss

You need to have a good relationship with your boss. Almost everything in your first years at work depends on this relationship. Like anything else in life, if you are lucky, getting on well with your boss can be very easy. If you are not lucky, it can be difficult and frustrating. The more you try to understand your relationship with the boss and the more you work on it, the better off you will be.

Bosses are all different and none of them is perfect. They are humans after all.

There was an excellent article published in the Harvard Business Review in 1980 called *'Managing Your Boss'*. It brought to light a whole new aspect of successful employees; essentially it said that a good relationship with a boss depends on both people – not just a good or bad boss.

The title *'Managing Your Boss'* makes the topic sound a bit like you are either brown-nosing or being politically subversive. Neither is the case. Try to think of it more as understanding what your boss wants, and how you can deliver it. The next few paragraphs include ideas from the article.

Psychologists have defined two types of behaviour that employees can adopt with their bosses. One is called *counter-dependence* and the other is over *dependence*. A boss naturally constrains an employee's freedom and judges his or her behaviour and performance. Essentially the boss tells you what to do, and different employees react to that in different ways.

Counter-dependent employees don't like authority figures. They do not like to be controlled or told what to do. They resent the direction of the boss. They view the boss as a hindrance to progress. In the most extreme cases, the boss is viewed as an enemy figure and the employee can feel persecuted by the boss. Usually there is no enemy or persecution, it's just an unfortunate juxtaposition of an authoritative boss and a counter-dependent employee, and they don't recognise what's going on. They could probably have a workable relationship if they were both aware if the issues.

Over-dependent employees are at the opposite end of the spectrum. They can view their boss as an all-knowing, all-seeing parent figure. They can view any feeling of disagreement with their boss as their own problem and will go to any length to agree with him or her, possibly losing sight of the real issues at hand.

It's very useful to try to get an idea of where you are on the spectrum of counter-dependence and over-dependence. We are all on it somewhere. Then you can look a bit more objectively at your reactions to your boss's requests, commands and comments to you. Remember – it's a continuous spectrum. You could be right in the middle or just slightly to one side or the other. Your own mood can swing your position on the line as well.

What is your immediate emotional reaction when someone tells you to do something?

If you think, *'Bugger off and do it yourself!'* then you could be counter-dependent. You could fight with your boss about issues that don't warrant an argument.

If you think, *'Oh yes, I'm sorry, how stupid of me for not thinking of that before,'* then you could be over-dependent. You might be prone to sweeping issues under the carpet just to keep the peace.

Personally I'm a bit counter-dependent. In my first years at work, I was naturally prone to think that my boss was a bit off the mark. But I knew that I was counter-dependent, so when I was about to argue with him I would stop, smile and say nothing. Then I would go away and look objectively at the issue at hand. Looking back fifteen years later I still think he was not very good at his job – but here's the important bit, it would have done me absolutely no good to say it to anyone, in fact it could have been career suicide.

The basis for a good relationship with your boss is to understand his or her expectations. As you get to know your boss try to answer the following questions:

- Does the boss like regular or infrequent information and updates?
- Does the boss prefer written or verbal reports?
- Does the boss tend to give people too much to do? If so, is it better to get someone else to help, to deliver it late, to work overtime or to tell him or her that you can't do it in time? (Note – it is very rarely an option to leave a task half finished.)
- Does the boss usually explain clearly what he or she wants? If not, then it's up to you to find out. Don't guess, get it wrong and deliver the wrong work.
- What sort of hours does the boss expect the team to work?
- What does your boss hate doing? Can you make it easier for him or her?
- Does the boss deal well with the emotions and personal issues of the employees? If not, then you might look elsewhere for emotional support. It does not help your relationship to cry on the boss's shoulder if he or she is not interested in personal issues.
- Does the boss trust people easily? You need to be dependable with any boss, but you have to be more visibly dependable with a boss who doesn't trust people easily. For example, it may be fine to ask a trusting boss to let you work at home sometimes – but not a boss who has problems trusting people.

- Is the boss's style formal or informal? Does he or she sit with you and talk to you as a co-worker or is there always a clear feeling of hierarchy when the boss is around. Follow the boss's style.

- What are the boss's pet topics? Make sure you know something about them. For example if the boss is an IT nut, then it will be harder for him or her to respect you if you are bad on the PC.

There are more examples we could write, but you should be getting the idea. Think about your boss's expectations. You could tactfully ask other employees in the department about how they see the boss's expectations – although it might be better to lay off the more personal questions. If the boss seems to labour any particular point, or area of work, then it is obviously important to him or her. Which means it is now important to you as well. And don't forget that if you are brighter than the boss, don't be too obvious about it. He or she will already know.

How to deal with a difficult boss

So many problems with 'difficult bosses' are really that the employee does not know what the boss wants, and the boss is not very good at explaining it. He or she may assume that employees will naturally work in the same way that he or she did as worker in the department. So what is needed is clarity, and you don't have to have a big explosion or an unhappy year to get clarity. You just have to ask.

Prepare your questions well, talk to other people if you trust them. Pick a good time when he or she is not very busy or visibly stressed and ask the boss to define exactly what he or she wants. Even better ask the boss to think about it and email it to you.

You may find yourself in a situation where you simply don't agree with something that your boss has asked you to do, or you think it could be done much better in a different way. If you find the right time and mood, then suggestions are okay, but remember that the boss is the boss, and it is your job to do what he or she says. You need to follow his or her lead even if you don't agree with it.

It is very rarely a good idea to go over your boss's head if you disagree on something. Your boss will never forgive you or trust you again. People who do challenge their boss so directly should have a good job offer up their sleeve.

Make an effort to understand what your boss does. Think about how you fit into his or her team and how he or she fits into the next level up. See the big picture, not just your own problem. Bosses' jobs are never easy and they will have even bigger bosses applying even bigger pressure. If you think your boss is being unreasonable, ask yourself why. What is your boss going through? What does he or she have to produce against an impossible deadline? Often with a broader perspective, harsh demands might not look so unreasonable after all.

I once read a book by David Lee Roth, the ex-lead singer of the rock band, Van Halen. It was no literary classic, but he did include a couple of excellent pieces of advice. Here's one of them. The wording is awful, but the message is very powerful.

'You are only as big as what you let get to you.'

As an employee you are paid to deal with problems. Your boss may be one of these problems. Deal with it. Don't become emotionally entwined. Don't let the problem control your mood or your attitude.

If you genuinely can't rise above the problem, then define some limits for yourself. What can you accept as a bad situation that will pass and what is unacceptable to you? You can write it down to help yourself be clear. (This is strictly for your eyes only). If your boss is going over the line it could be better to end this bad relationship and move on than to stay and fight.

It seldom hurts to get another job offer. You don't have to take it. Have a look around (but don't tell anyone at work that you are looking). If you find a good offer and the problems with your boss are no better, then it might be a good idea to move. Make a fresh start and build a reputation in the new firm. If you can't get another offer that attracts you, then you can look to move to another department within the company.

Note – if the problems with your boss are related to unwelcome sexual advances, then go straight to your head of HR and tell him or her. No one has to put up with this anymore. The head of HR will stop it immediately. They have the power to discipline or sack people who cause these sorts of problems.

Chapter twenty-two summary

- ☑ **You depend very heavily on your boss, especially in the early years at work.**
- ☑ **A good relationship depends on both of you, not just on whether he or she is a good boss.**
- ☑ **The relationship is much easier if you understand what he or she does and what he or she expects.**
- ☑ **Be very cautious about challenging the boss – it usually ends up damaging the all-important relationship.**

Next ➔➔

To get on in a firm, you need to understand its culture.

23

Cultural Awareness

Culture can be a vague notion, everyone talks about it, but it can be hard to pin culture down.

A good way to describe culture is *'the way we do things around here'*. If you hear people saying, *'we don't do it like that here,'* or *'we prefer to look at it like this,'* that's culture. Listen to it carefully. When people say things like that, it is often a polite way of saying, *'get your act together and start playing on our team, not your own.'* If you hear comments like these quite often, then you are probably ignoring the company culture. If you hear them say, *'Yeah, we always do that too,'* then you are on the ball.

Here are some pointers for you to start to think about culture. Remember that every company is different. The tips your big brother can give you from his company could be out of place in yours if the culture is very different. Put some effort in to understanding the culture of your firm. It is really important for a good start in your career.

- What time do people arrive, take lunch and leave? Your boss and immediate co-workers are the most important. Put in the same hours they do or a bit more. Do people come and go at different times on different days or is it regimented 9:00 to 5:45 and not a minute different? Do what the others do. Do they do overtime, do they take work home and do they work weekends?

- Dress – is it formal or informal? Look at shoes as well as suits, ties and so on. Dress at least as formally as others, or a bit more formally at first.

- Do the managers and employees socialise together? If they do, then you must as well.

- Language and conversation topics – do people talk in normal social type conversations or is it formal with lots of business terms? Follow the norm, and at first be a little more polite and conservative.

- Do people inform you about what is going on? Sometimes it's hard for new employees to know and that makes them feel a bit unwanted. In some cultures it's fine to ask regularly about what's happening in the office and in others it's not. Ask other recent employees how they find out what's going on.

The culture of schools and universities is very different from office culture. You used to compete against everyone for better marks, you used to get feedback on your performance for every piece of work that you did and your social behaviour did not matter very much. Now you need to help each other all the time, you get feedback once every six months and your social behaviour is just as important as your work itself. It's quite a different game, and the quicker you get accustomed to the new culture, the more successful you will be.

Keep looking for telltales of culture all the time – that's how the people in the firm can accept you quickly. Pay more attention to the way the popular and successful employees act. They are the ones who fit in with the culture. Try not to spend too much time with people who are obvious misfits. You will be seen as a trainee misfit, regardless of how you really are.

Chapter twenty-three summary

- ☑ **Culture can be a vague notion, but you need to understand it.**
- ☑ **If you don't learn your company's culture then you risk being a square peg in a round hole – not good for the peg or the hole.**
- ☑ **Pay attention to 'how we do things around here'.**
- ☑ **Company culture is generally very different to school or university culture – if you expect the change you should be able to adjust much more quickly.**

Next ➔➔

Business is done in teams. Some teams work and some don't. The next chapter will help you understand why.

24

Team Skills

Most people will agree that the times when they have been most successful were when they were in a team that got on well, had fun, worked hard in the day, and went out together in the evening. It can be as if a special spice suddenly enters your work life. Teams where everyone is arguing all the time, and the people don't enjoy the task are a nightmare. Every minute is painful. When you are in a team, try as hard as you can to make it a good experience for everyone.

We are going to look at teams from two perspectives. First we look at the four stages in the life of a team and second, we look at the roles that each individual can play in a team.

When you have a good feel for where the team is as a whole, and a good feel for where you are within the team, it makes team life easier, more fun and much more successful.

These two perspectives are entry level 'team science'. The aim is to enable you to see what is going on objectively. There is a great deal of work out there on how to set up and manage teams. Different companies and industries often have their own cultures and fashions regarding knowledge on teams. Ask your training department what they use and recommend, if you want to look into teams further. If you read the wrong stuff and try to apply it, you could end up grating against your company culture.

The four stages in the life of a team are:

- the welcome
- first blood
- getting on together
- production.

These four stages are a naturally occurring result of group dynamics. Stick five people in a room and this is what happens.

When a team first forms everyone is usually eager, polite and wants to dive into all the issues and tasks. We call this the **Welcome**. It's about learning to be together and learning the initial parts of the work. Each person wants to express his or her ideas. There will be good suggestions and bad ones. Go with the good ones and don't worry about the bad ones – they're always there. Listen to other people's ideas as well as pushing your own. The Welcome can be quite short, perhaps not more than a couple of meetings.

The second stage is **First Blood**. This sounds a bit dramatic and it can be. The team members start to test out their roles within the team. They start trying to assert themselves. Each team member tries to push his or her own ideas or approaches and when two ideas contradict each other arguments can break out.

First blood can be nothing more than a couple of raised eyebrows that are forgotten in two minutes, or it can be the complete downfall and failure of the team. It depends on the individuals and how well the team is being run. A skilled team leader can guide a team through First Blood without any blood. A bad leader or no leader can result in a big mess that is never resolved. If tempers are fraying in the First Blood stage, remember to remain totally professional. Don't be drawn into a personal battle.

The third stage in the life of a team is **Getting on Together**. Once the roles are formed and the basic approach to the work is set there is less to argue about. If you were involved in any arguments in First Blood now is the time to be friendly to your former opponent.

Stage four is **Production**. This is when the team finally produces the goods. The roles and approaches are set, the teething troubles are over. Make sure you deliver the work needed from your role. Try to help others if they are having problems in their tasks. Think about the end product – it needs to be tied-up neatly before handing over. Think about how to make sure your contribution is noted (but tactfully).

Team roles

Most teams are made up of people working in various roles. If the roles are clear and they fit together well, the team is more likely to succeed. When you enter a team, make sure you identify all the roles. Sometimes they will be explicit, everyone is told what role they play, and sometimes they will not, everyone has to work it out amongst themselves.

The team leader

The leader is usually assigned before the team is even formed. The best thing a leader can do is to get the team to work together well early on. He or she needs to sort out what there is to be done and who is going to do it. Then each team member can start efficiently with his or her task.

Some leaders try to do all the work themselves. If that was practical then they would not need a team – these people are not very good leaders. Support them and let them begin to trust you and they should relax a bit and start to use the team properly.

Other leaders only focus on the tasks and ignore the people. They talk all day about the technical issues but pay no attention to the team members or the team roles. They can be hard to work for. Don't take it personally if they are abrupt with you.

At the opposite extreme you can get leaders who are lovely to everyone but don't really know what to do in terms of the task. If they are smart they will realise this and have a right hand man or woman who does know the task. This set up can work very well. If they don't have a right hand person then it's a mess. Lots of hugs and kisses but nothing to give to the big boss at the end of the day. If this happens, then be clear with the leader about what you think your task is, and deliver it – even if the others are not doing very much.

The team worker

Your main role will probably be a Team Worker in your first year(s) at work. The team boss should explain what tasks he or she wants you to perform. If he or she doesn't tell you then make your best guess and check it out. Think about how your task interacts with the other team members. Do you require information from them? If so ask them politely how the things you need fit in with the rest of their work. Don't barge in and say I need this, that and the other because the boss said so.

Do other people require input from you? If so, ask them what they need. Let them know when you should be able to give it to them.

If you really don't know what's going on, then ask. Better in private than in front of the whole group. Companies value people who ask when they don't know what to do. Have a good think about it first; see if you can work it out on your own. But if not then ask – it's so much better than to waste time doing the wrong things, or even worse, nothing.

Have conviction in your role as a really good team worker. It is the best foundation you can have for a great career.

The team expert

Quite often the leader will not be the most technically expert person on the team. Experts are brought in to do the most technical tasks, or to teach the others the necessary information or techniques. There is no great secret of how to deal with the expert. Listen, ask questions when you need to. Take notes, it looks good and helps you remember what the expert said.

The team outsider

Sometimes there's a person in the team who is shunned by the other team members. This is almost always because of some interpersonal problem or argument, either within this team or a previous one.

Don't become a team outsider. Don't think that you can just weather it for the duration of one team and then get on the right track in the next one – there may not be a next team and if there is, a previous outsider comes in at a great disadvantage. If you ever feel yourself becoming an outsider to the team then you need to change your attitude very fast.

If someone else is an obvious outsider then don't join in the bullying, and don't visibly support the outsider in arguments. Be pleasant and neutral.

The team diplomat

There can be a team member who takes it upon him or herself to keep the harmony of the team going. This is more likely to be a woman than a man – but it can be either. It is rare that anyone has this role officially, but it can actually be extremely important to the success of the team. If you see that someone spends quite a lot of effort to help other team members get on and to smooth out arguments then take note of what they are doing (especially if it involves you directly). Don't ignore this as warm and cuddly stuff. A good team diplomat can spot a head-to-head coming and avert it in 30 seconds. It can save weeks of arguing and problems.

The team secretary or administrator

Some teams have a dedicated secretary or admin worker. Quite often even if you are not a career secretary you may be asked to perform this role for teams early in your career. Again, after years in education this can be a frustrating prospect. If so then try to change your perspective of what team work is all about. Eighty percent of it is not about technical brilliance. It's about getting things done, and the team admin person can be crucial in getting things done.

Use the opportunity to observe all the team roles. Remember what we said in the section about the Rookie Year – even if the tasks are not that challenging do them well – then you will get the chance to do something better.

The team objective

Always keep in mind the overall objective for the team. It's easy to be sidetracked by interesting red herrings or to allow personal agendas to creep into teams. Know what the output for the team is and know how you contribute to it.

Chapter twenty-four summary

☑ **Teams are the driving force behind many businesses. They are where the work is actually done.**

☑ **Some teams work well and others don't, and usually the success or failure is within the control of the team members.**

☑ **Be aware of the four stages in the life of a team, and all the different roles.**

☑ **Identify your role and how it fits in with the rest of the team and make sure you deliver your part – whatever else is going on.**

Next ➔➔

It's easy to think that if your technical knowledge is good, then your career will be easy. Actually, it's not that simple – in the nest chapter, we investigate why.

25

Knowledge

Don't fall into the trap where you think that if you know the technology of your job then that's all you need. People who do that stagnate at quite a low level in most professions.

The difference between an outstanding employee and an average one is rarely just down to a better knowledge of the job technology. The outstanding employee is much better in all the other areas – company culture, team work, communication, presentation and so on.

Think about knowledge in broader terms. We break it up into five categories:

- job-specific technical
- job-specific process
- general business
- economic, political, social
- information technology.

Here are some tips on how to approach knowledge in each category:

Job-specific technical knowledge

For some jobs, the specific technical knowledge is more important than others. Brain surgeons need to know a lot about brains. The more specifics you know, the better. In any job, make sure your job specific knowledge is at least as good as the others around you. If it is not then it might be worth spending a couple of evenings a week reading up on the technology of your job.

Job-specific process knowledge

This is knowledge of the process of how work is done in your firm or department. Who does what and then gives it to whom. Essentially it's what the middle managers of a company do, they organise the process of the work.

In some companies, it's all written down in procedures manuals. They are about as exciting as chewing chalk but it's good to browse them. In other firms it is never written down – just passed on from manager to manager. The faster you pick it up, the faster you are eligible to be a manager. Keep your eyes and ears open to what is going on around you.

There is a big picture for every company. What does the firm do as a whole and how does each employee contribute? Get to know the big picture of your firm, and how you fit into it.

General business knowledge

Reading books is the best way to build your general business knowledge. There are many good books around, and lots of bad ones. Ask people at work what they have read that was interesting and relevant. Good books on people skills and your approach to every-day work are always useful. You can use your new knowledge immediately because you deal with people every day. *'The Seven Habits of Highly Effective People'* by Stephen Covey is a good example. Books on high-flown corporate strategy can be attractive, but the MD doesn't usually bring in all the new recruits to set the next five years' strategy for the firm. Stick to what you can use to start with. The more you read the better. Try to read what your boss and colleagues are reading.

Economic, political and social knowledge

This comes down to reading the paper, reading *The Economist*, watching the news and talking with generally informed people. In some jobs it is very important and in others it's not. As a minimum, you need to be informed enough that you don't look out of touch in conversation. You can get that from scanning the headlines every day or so. Further than that is up to you. I found it more useful putting my time into business books, professional societies and networking than reading every single column of the paper.

IT knowledge

We talked about this in the interview section of the book. Here's a recap. You need to know Windows, Word and Outlook as an absolute minimum to work in any office environment. If you don't know these programs then learn them quickly.

MS Excel is essential if your job is numerical, and PowerPoint is very useful. Your job will probably involve other software – if so try to learn it as fast as possible. People notice very quickly who is good on the PC and who is not, and it's another aspect of that all-important reputation.

Here's a quick example of what knowledge can do for you.

> I started as a design engineer, but I read quite a lot of business books. People noticed and that got me onto a company Think Tank, which got me into the Corporate Development Department, which got me a job as a management consultant (via an MBA), which paid way more cash than I would have ever earned as an engineer. It all started with broadening my knowledge base into areas that I had not studied before.

Chapter twenty-five summary

☑ **Take a broad view of your knowledge and think about where you can brush up.**

☑ **Don't assume that you necessarily need the same approach as your co-workers.**

☑ **If you have the energy to keep on studying then devise a plan that gives you a well balanced knowledge in all five areas.**

Next ➔➔

To make money, a business has to sell. Be aware of this and learn how to do it.

26

Selling, Persuading and Influencing

People think that Bill Gates became the richest man in the world because his computer programs were better than anyone else's. In fact they were not. Apple had better technology in the early days of personal computers. The difference was that Gates could sell. He could spot the market and knew how to persuade the people to buy his product.

You probably won't be asked to start selling anything to clients early in your career, but you will need to sell your ideas to colleagues and persuade your boss to give you a pay rise. It is always very useful in business to be able to sell or persuade.

Focus on what your audience wants. You want to sell your idea or product or persuade the audience to your point of view. Put yourself in their shoes. Figure out what they actually want. When you are explaining or persuading, concentrate on the areas of your idea that fit with what they are after. Don't go on about something that you find interesting if they don't. They won't buy it.

There is a lot of talk in sales literature about the difference between benefits and features.

A **feature** is something you thought of or designed. 'Extra hot wash cycle' is a feature. A **benefit** is something that the buyer wants. They don't care about what you designed; they care about what they want. They want Johnny's cricket trousers to be virgin white on Sunday afternoon. White trousers are the benefit. They don't care how it happens. If you sell how to get the trousers white they buy, if you sell hot wash they don't. That's the concept of features and benefits. Try to think in terms of benefits. How does your idea benefit the audience?

When you are selling, persuading or influencing, you are asking people to believe in what you say. You are asking people to believe in you. Your delivery must convey confidence, self-belief and enthusiasm. If you are not very enthusiastic about your idea or product then why should they be?

Here is how to pull it off:

- Rehearse what you are going to say beforehand.

- You must adopt confident body language for the entire encounter. This means no folded arms or crossed legs. Stand up and stand tall. Lots of eye contact. Don't wring your hands together or hold them in front of your crotch. Use big open hand gestures to emphasise your best points. Shoulders back, lots of body, then people can see that you are confident.

- Speak clearly and reasonably slowly even if you are nervous. Use a deeper tone rather than a higher one. Breathe deeply – don't pant between sentences.

- Speak with as much enthusiasm as you can. Let people see how much you enjoy the product or idea.

There is a balance between understanding your audience and using this strong, confident style of presentation. Some sales people cut out the listening part and just use the strong stuff. It's called hard selling. It worked twenty years ago for double-glazing salesmen, but it rarely works now. Most people have seen it all before. Use a combination of attention to your audience and confident selling technique – that will get you much further.

Chapter twenty-six summary

☑ Even if you are not selling products to clients at work you still have to 'sell' ideas and persuade people.

☑ Think about what they want as well as what you want. Why should they be interested in your idea?

☑ If you find out what turns them on, then you can offer your idea or point in a manner that is much more likely to be accepted.

Next ➔➔

You will spend more than half your time at work communicating. In the next chapter, we look at how to do it effectively.

27

Communication Skills

Verbal communication

When some people talk, everyone wants to listen. How can a speaker achieve that? There is a common mistake made when people are talking. Some people think that to make others listen all they have to do is to make the cleverest point in the conversation. 'I'm right, so people have to listen!' Well, there is a bit more to it than that.

If you listen to other people then they will listen to you. If you think about what they want, then they may have some patience to think about what you want. Otherwise they might not.

Before you launch into what you want to say, pause for a moment. Look at your audience. Think about who they are and what they want. Ask yourself how your point looks from their perspective. See yourself through their eyes. Find some common ground between what you want and what they want and then make your point in a way that is as attractive as possible to them. It sounds a little bit like the material in the previous section on selling, and that's no coincidence.

Many people in the past have stuck with the bulldozer approach to getting their points across. They make their point with only themselves in mind and have little care for the listeners. This approach can work if you are speaking down the hierarchy. People below you don't have much choice except to listen. However this approach can be a disaster across or up the hierarchy. People don't want to be lectured.

So, when you are about to start talking, consider these factors.

- Form your ideas in a concise and organised manner.
- Look at who your audience is.
- Ask yourself, what do they get out of the points?
- Try to involve something in your approach that is attractive to them.
- Then make your points, and listen to what they say in reply.

We talk quite a lot about listening throughout this section of the book. Here are some tips for active listening.

- Listen without interrupting – even if you think it's all rubbish.
- Make eye contact every now and then with the speaker to show you are still interested and listening.
- Say 'yes' or 'yeah' or whatever affirmative phrase you use.
- There is nothing more flattering in the world than someone's complete positive attention. Pay attention and you should see very soon how the speaker appreciates it.

Situations where you want to listen to someone politely but you disagree completely with what they are saying can be difficult. Our advice is that you still listen to the points without interrupting – simply out of courtesy. Then give your own counter points in a logical and structured manner. Hopefully, whomever you are talking to will also listen and you can have an intelligent conversation.

Written communication

When you have to write a report, a letter or a memo, try the following approach:

- Plan the main points in your mind, then note down the titles of each point with some brief ideas.
- Plan to get your meaning across in the minimum number of pages. People are busy and they don't want to read a twenty-page saga when one page would give them all they need to know.
- Put the points in an order that flows, this is your structure. If the points are good but the structure is bad then the points are all lost. Take time over your structure.

- Think about your reader, what will he or she get out of your text? Make sure there is something in it for them.
- Write the text for your points, keeping your reader's perspective in mind. Put something in the first sentence or paragraph that will grab their attention.
- Put a link sentence at the end of each point to lead into the next one.
- Write an introduction at the beginning.
- Write a summary at the end.
- Print it out and read it through very carefully. There are always mistakes even using spell checkers and grammar checkers.
- Read it through to make sure the words flow. Read it out loud. If you have to stop or pause when reading your own text then the wording is probably poor. Most writers have to change their wording from the first script.
- If possible, get a friend or co-worker to read through your text before you send it.

Emails

There are very many terrible emails written in offices. A bad email is a hit on your reputation. You don't want that. Plan the text of an email just as you would for a letter or formal memo.

There is a tendency for emails to appear much more blunt or even rude to the reader than was intended by the writer. It's a result of the brevity of emails and the lack of any formality. A formally written letter has implied courtesy – the writer has taken the trouble to adhere to the etiquette of written communication. An email has no implied courtesy and it's very easy to come across as abrupt. Sometimes I imagine that my fingers are like little hammers bashing away at the keyboard when writing an email – I keep it in mind to soften it up. Always make sure your business emails are as polite as possible.

Try to send fewer rather than more emails. A busy professional, especially a manager, can easily receive fifty or more emails in a day. It can literally take hours to respond to them, which gets in the way of other work. Try to send a fewer, more relevant emails rather than lots of little comments about every idea that crossed your mind. Make them concise rather than wordy. If an email has to be long then use an attachment.

Different offices have different policies about using your business email for personal mail. They do have the right to look at what you're sending/receiving and most IT departments perform checks. Find out if it's acceptable before giving your business email address to all your friends.

NEVER send/receive/look at fruity pictures on your work PC. People get fired for it. Network systems can be set up to automatically inform the IT department of any such material coming in or out. Avoid getting on any joke groups with your business email if you can. If someone sends you a racist joke, it's on your PC and you could be associated with it whether you like it or not.

Chapter twenty-seven summary

☑ **It has been said that no one ever wants to listen – they're just waiting for a chance to talk.**

☑ **If you listen to other people and have good reasons as to why they should listen to you then they might give you their genuine attention.**

☑ **Think about how your point sounds to them before you say it.**

☑ **What do they get out of it? Plan your points so that you give them something they want as well as getting across what you want.**

☑ **When writing use a structured approach. Don't just tap the keys until all your ideas are on the page somewhere and then send it.**

☑ **Make the points flow, make the text read easily and check everything through before you send it, letters, memos, emails, whatever.**

28

Decisions

Successful business people must be able to make decisions. Most managers have to make decisions with less time and less information than they would like and they can never be sure of the outcome.

This can be a bit daunting at first. You may come to a point where you need to make a decision but you don't feel that you really know enough about the options to have a good chance of getting it right. But you need to be seen to make decisions.

Here are six steps to help you put some structure into your decision-making. (Use your judgement as to whether you need all of the steps depending on how involved or important the decision is).

1. Do all your **research** including facts and figures and look for reports or stories of similar situations so that you can see what decision was made there. Find out everything that you can on your own first, and then ask others for information if you need to.

2. Note down all the **pros and cons** and **risks** surrounding the decision. It helps to see it all on paper. Some decisions will be very obvious from the facts, you don't have to do too much thinking, and others will be much more of a judgement call. Take more time to think if it is a judgement call.

3. Take a **preliminary decision**. Now ask yourself how likely is it that you got it right? Very few issues are black and white. When you are dealing with shades of grey, it is useful to know how sure you are. Even a guess at the probability of being right can be more

helpful than nothing at all. High level decision makers employ mathematical models to simulate probability of being right.

4. Look at what happens if the decision turns out to be wrong. If someone is going to lose a lot of money, or worse, then you might want to do some more research.

5. **Check the decision** with a trusted friend or co-worker if you can. A second opinion can quite often help you identify something that you have missed or it can bring a new perspective to the decision.

6. **Take the final decision**, and have all the back up ready if anyone asks for it – supporting information, pros and cons, probability of being right and consequences. If things do not go as well as you hoped, you may need to be able to show that you made a sound decision based on the information available at the time. Hindsight can be very revealing – be prepared to show how thorough you were.

Here's a story about decisions from early in my own career:

I was working on a petrol additives plant in Wyoming and we were having trouble with the main compressor. We could not get it started up. Starting a big industrial compressor can be tricky – the electric motor gets hotter every time you try, and if you have more than three aborted attempts you have to wait a long time for it to cool down before you can try again. The motors are huge – this one would have filled a two-car garage. Waiting for it to cool down means hours of lost production and money down the drain. We had been trying to start it all morning and the mood was getting a bit fraught. No one was really in charge; we had six engineers standing over one console, all giving their best advice.

We went ahead with the next attempt to start the compressor. The electric current feeding the motor was looking a little bit high. We reached the critical moment where you either shut it down deliberately to save time before the next start, or let it go, in which case it either starts or overheats. The room went quiet. The guy working the console asked what he should do. The room stayed quiet. The current to the motor was still building up, and the compressor was starting to pump – but very slowly. It was a fifty-fifty decision to shut it down or let it run. It could have gone either way and no one was prepared to make the decision. No one wanted to get it wrong.

The guy on the console started to panic – *'I'm shutting down, I'm shutting down!'* Everyone was looking a bit lost as they watched his hand move to the big red abort button. Except me. I was looking at the electric current to the motor – which was starting to flatten out. *'Let it run!'* said a voice all of a sudden. Half a second later, I realised it was mine. Six pairs of eyes hit me. I was half the age of most of the engineers there. *'Look – it's starting to pump.'* The eyes moved to the console and then slowly back to me. They didn't look too friendly either. *'Look – it's taking the feed gas.'* The voice carried on, a little higher pitched this time. The current was still high but the compressor was starting to pump, which meant we might get away with it. I was starting to sweat now – and it's very cold in winter in Wyoming. Then all of a sudden the big machine took the feed properly and the current to the motor started dropping. The compressor had started. Six pairs of cold eyes transformed into six big hands patting me on the back. Twelve lungs full of tightly held breath exhaled all at once. *'He did it!'* someone shouted *'He did it!'*

I could have crashed the site truck that afternoon and still have been the hero. And all I had done was to make a decision when no one else wanted to. I was a bit lucky as well – the compressor could have overheated and shut itself down. But what mattered was that someone had stood up and taken the decision. I think I would still have come out all right if it had shut down. The fact was that the others were too scared to say anything and they were more than a bit impressed that a 24-year old engineer from 'Little Old England' was prepared to put his neck on the line and make a decision.

I didn't use a well structured approach to that particular decision – I had no idea that I was about to make it in the first place, but I did write a guide to starting the compressor that was well structured and would allow the next person to evaluate the options a bit more clearly at any given moment in the start up procedure.

You should find that with more years of experience, the gathering of information and intelligent weighing-up of the odds becomes easier. But there is always a bit of a leap of faith when we have to make a decision. Being able to make that leap doesn't come from textbooks or statistical tables. It comes from you.

Chapter twenty-eight summary

- ☑ **All successful business people are able to make decisions. They don't always get them right, but they do take them.**
- ☑ **Try to use a structured approach to decisions.**
- ☑ **If the decision is important then weigh up the odds of getting it wrong and look at the consequences.**
- ☑ **Serious consequences may make it worthwhile doing a bit more research.**
- ☑ **Keep the backup information for the decisions that you make. If a decision turns out to have been wrong you might need to show that you made a reasonable decision given the information available at the time.**

Next ➔➔

We talked about networking in terms of finding job openings. Now we will look at your networking once you have a job.

29

Networking

Every successful business person has a wide network of business friends and associates. Remember the old saying 'it's not what you know it's who you know' – a cliché, but a good one. When people are wondering who they can call to join a new team, or to solve a particular problem, you want them to think of you.

Meet as many people as you can. Always carry your business cards around with you. Try to meet people outside your immediate team or department at work. We said earlier that company clubs or societies are a good place for this.

Most lines of work have professional societies that you can join. This might not be the wildest way to spend your evenings, but they are a fantastic place to create a network of colleagues.

Often they will have a meeting or dinner every month. Go along and meet some people. It can be hard at first if you go on your own, everyone seems to know everyone else and may not be just standing there waiting to talk to you. Catch people in a pause and be really open, just say something like, *'Hello, I'm Jo from Burg's Chemicals, who do you work for?'* Most people are friendly at these sorts of dos and will be happy to include you in their conversation. If you go every month to start with it, doesn't take long to make some friends. Try to do favours for your new network buddies.

Chapter twenty-nine summary

- ☑ **Hardly anyone rises to success on his or her own.**
- ☑ **Create a network of colleagues and help each other out as much as you can.**
- ☑ **Try to meet people in similar lines of work outside your company as well as inside.**
- ☑ **Professional societies are ideal for this.**

Next ➔➔

Some people are well organised. The next chapter is a brief reminder to make sure that you are also well organised.

30

Organisation

Get used to planning everything that you do. Rushing into things usually ends up slower because you have to re-think what you are up to half way through. Take a few minutes every morning to plan your day. Who needs to receive your work and how do they expect it to arrive?

Have a clear idea of your timing for the day and the week. Keep a diary and make sure you always know when your meetings and appointments are. Never be late.

Many organisations rely on the employees filling out timesheets every week for the company accounts. Timesheets are really important. If you don't fill your timesheet in on time the firm can't bill the clients. It is a major responsibility for your boss to get his or her department's timesheets submitted every week. Don't let him or her down.

Some people are naturally tidy and some are not. What you do with your clothes at home is up to you, but your desk needs to be tidy. If your desk looks a mess then people assume that your work is the same, not good for the old reputation.

The same goes for any written work that you produce. Technical people often think that if the numbers are right then who cares about the presentation? The answer is that everyone else does. Everything you produce needs to look nice, even if you feel it's a pain to do it. It's better to take a little more time to get things right and presentable than it is to hand over untidy or unfinished work. It's easier for some people than others – but either way you have to do it. There is a term 'Closure'. Bring closure to all your work.

31

Sex in the Office

Upright, moralistic and politically correct readers should perhaps think twice about reading this section. The rest should think about reading it twice.

My dad used to be Managing Director of a large engineering firm. An employee came into his office one day looking a bit sheepish. He said,

'Er, Roger, there is something I should ask you. I'm, er, well, er, sort of seeing your secretary, if you know what I mean. Er, you don't mind, do you?'

My dad is more of the succinct type than a real conversationalist. He looked up from his report and said,

'Not in office time, not on office furniture. That's all, thank you.' And then carried on reading.

Sex in the office – tips for the girls

Men will view you slightly differently once they know you are having or have had an affair with a guy at the office. They feel that they know something more about you than your normal business persona. It's completely unfair, totally sexist and very outdated, but it's unfortunately true.

I had a girlfriend at the office once who was adamant that no one should know about us. I didn't like it – I thought she wasn't very proud of me. Actually that wasn't the case at all. She knew how men form their opinions of people. She was doing the right thing. If people know you are with a guy at the office, there can be an undertone that you get things easier than everyone else, especially if he is higher up the ladder than you. Our advice is to do what you want, but make sure it's kept quiet. Really quiet.

Tips for the guys

It's never a great idea to lull a nice young lady into the false assumption that you care about her innermost desires, lure her into bed and have some fun, and then do an Olympic-pace runner. In the office it is a major blunder. How far can you run? Two floors up? Twenty yards round the corner? Either way you have to be at your desk before the boss gets back from lunch.

Torrid, on office furniture, in office time affairs do go on, but they are rare. A lady risks more damage to her reputation than you do to in such an affair. If you feel adequately Machiavellian to try to strike up such a relationship, then make sure you have radar-like intuition. Change your middle name to 'Stealthy' before you start.

Tips for both

Relationships lead to getting married or splitting up. If you get married then great. But if you split up then you can land yourself with a whole new bunch of problems at work. If you value your reputation, then try to choose a partner who is as professional about his or her career as you are about yours. You would not believe some of the things that go on after an office affair splits up.

Here's an example – totally crazy, but absolutely one hundred percent true.

The company lawyer at my old firm was a bit of a ladies' man. He had been having an affair with a lady who worked in the firm. Apparently they had fallen out and she was not very happy with him. The gory details never came to light but it ended up with the most unbelievable office scene I had ever heard of. She still had a key to his house. She went there and took his gun (I was working in Houston, Texas at the time, where everyone has a gun). She came into the building went straight up to his office, pointed the gun at him and told him to apologise for what he had done. He wasn't feeling terribly apologetic, so he ran. Just legged it.

She followed him, still brandishing his gun, and screaming. They ran all the way down the corridor outside the MD's and Directors' offices, down the fire escape and out into the car park. It was unbelievable – like a combination of Punch and Judy and Rambo. She didn't shoot him in the end, so we assumed he must eventually have apologised.

As we said earlier – it's a marriage or a split. Either way, make sure you know what you are getting into before it's too late!

Do what you want but keep it quiet from everyone else at work, before, during and after your dangerous liaison. Don't turn up in the same car, or walking hand-in-hand together through the front door. Don't sit on top of each other at lunch gazing into each other's eyes, and if you are bold enough to chance a quick one in the corner meeting room, make sure the door is locked and no one else has a key!

Chapter thirty-one summary

☑ **Don't kiss and tell.**

Next ➔➔

Coming back to a slower pace, let's think about problem solving.

32

Problem Solving

Bosses don't want to hear about problems, they usually have enough of their own. But they do want to hear about solutions, sweeping important issues under the carpet doesn't help. Always try to think in terms of solutions not problems.

Often we can be faced with a big problem and it can be hard to see where to start. It can feel a bit overwhelming to try to solve the whole issue at once. So don't. Break it up into smaller problems that you can solve and then fit the solutions back together.

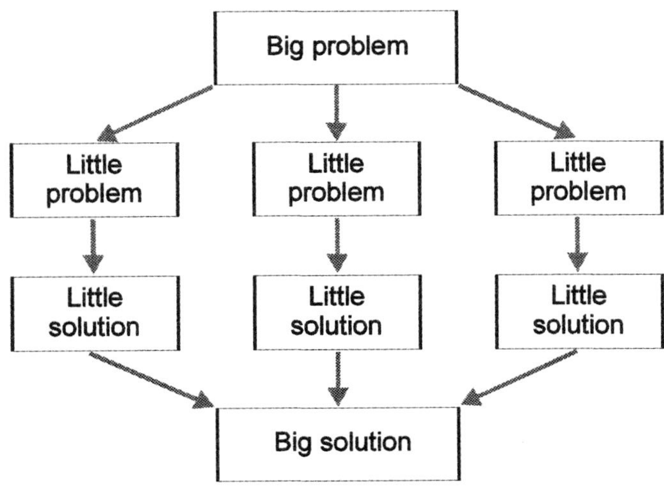

Here's an example (it should sound familiar).

You need to choose a career. Where do you start? Well, you don't try to come up with an answer in one step. You think about who you are, you think about your qualifications, you think about your dreams and so on. These are smaller problems that you can solve. If one of the little problems still seems hard to tackle then break it down further. Thinking about who you are is difficult. So break it down into personality, desires and talents. Now you're at a level where you can find answers. Then you fit all the solutions together step by step.

If you end up with a lot of smaller problems on different levels then use a diagram to keep track of how it all fits together.

Here's a last thought about problems. Write a list of your own problems at work. Then write a list of your boss's problems. Throw the first one in the bin and work on solutions for the second one. It'll get you further in the long run.

Chapter thirty-two summary

☑ **Don't go to your boss with problems. Go with solutions.**

☑ **If a problem is too big to tackle in one go, break it down in to smaller problems and solve them.**

☑ **Worry more about your boss's problems than your own.**

Next ➔➔

We come to the last chapter – it's time for you to think about your ambition.

33

Ambition

What do you want and how far are you prepared to go to get it?

I had dinner with an old university friend a couple of years ago. She always worked really hard; she got a first class degree at Cambridge and then became an accountant. She is very ambitious. She moved to an investment bank – in fact the richest one in London. We were talking about holidays and she said she had only had three days off so far that year. I asked if they were difficult about taking all your holiday time at the bank. She said no, she didn't mean holiday, she meant three days in total she had not been at work. It was June when we met. That means she worked eight weeks solid, no weekends or bank holidays, and had just one day off, and then did it again, twice. We finished dinner at about 10 pm. She paid, because she's nice and then she went back to the office. She makes incredible money; her Christmas bonus was probably the same as my salary.

People who get to the top are prepared to go the extra mile. They are prepared to stay late every night, work weekends, cancel holidays, phone their partner to say they won't be home for dinner and to find a new partner when the old one is fed up with having dinner alone three nights a week.

Different firms have different cultures surrounding how hard you need to work. Try to decide for yourself how ambitious you want to be and see how it fits into the culture of your firm. In some places if you stay 20 minutes after the day officially, ends you are a hero. In other places if you leave before 9pm, you are a lightweight.

Some people find it very useful to be objective about their ambitions. Where do you want to be 15 years from now? Do you want a massive salary and a lot of respect in the office, or do you want a comfortable salary and time to spend with your family? It is uncommon to have both. Try writing down what you want to achieve, and then have a look at what you think you need to do in order to achieve it.

If you are really ambitious then you need to work for the sort of firm that puts effort into developing its employees. If you are in a firm full of grey faces that complain about lack of career opportunity, then you will probably have a difficult time becoming a high flyer quickly. Do people receive good training at your firm? Do the more able employees get promoted quickly? Does anyone ever talk to you about your career objectives and how you can achieve them? If not then think about moving to another firm.

Whatever your job is, do it well. It is easy to have your head in the clouds preparing for a great future and to lose interest in the everyday work. Don't make that mistake.

Keep your eyes and ears open all the time. Look for opportunities, and when they arrive, take them. And above all make sure that you are enjoying your work. Forty years is a long time, too long to spend doing something you don't like.

Work hard, be friendly and be honest and you should go every bit as far as you want to.

Good luck for your future from all of us.

Further Reading

Ace Your Case, Wet Feet Press, http://www.wetfeet.com
All About Psychological Tests and Assessment Centres, Jack van Minden, Management Books 2000
Beware those who ask for Feedback, Richard A Moran, HarperBusiness
Body Language, David Langram and The Diagram Group, HaperCollins Publishers
Do What You Are, Paul Tieger & Barbara Barron Tieger, Little, Brown & Co.
Great Answers to Tough Interview Questions, Martin Yate, Kogan Page
Hire Education, John Hobart, Lighthouse Point Press
How to be a People Magnet, Leil Lowndes, Thorsons
How to Win Friends and Influence People, Dale Carnegie
Managing Your Career, Harvard Business Review, HBS Press
Managing Your Career, Rebecca Tee, Essential Managers, Dorling Kindersley
Reject Me, I Love It, John Furman, Possibility Press
Seven Habits of Highly Successful People, Stephen Covey
The Super Teams Book, Mike Pegg, Management Books 2000

About the Author

Neil Thompson has Bachelor's and Master's degrees in Chemical Engineering at Cambridge University.

He spent the first five years of his career working in the petrochemicals and oil and gas industry based in Houston, Texas. He became interested in people in organisations early on. He took part in the Think Tank for his firm's future strategy at the age of 26 and presented and published original material on effective teams in petrochemical projects in the USA.

He then moved back to the UK, spent a year with Kvaerner Corporate Development and took a year out to study for an MBA at Cranfield.

After the MBA he worked for KPMG Management Consultancy based in London.

He has lived and worked in Germany, Spain, France and South Korea as well as the UK and the USA.

Neil has been involved in recruitment and job search throughout his career and has experience sitting on both sides of the interview table.

Index

Index